Amusement Parks

An American Guidebook

by

John Norris

and

Joann Norris

McFarland & Company, Inc., Publishers
Jefferson, North Carolina, and London

Library of Congress Cataloguing-in-Publication Data

Norris, John, 1944–
  Amusement parks.

  Includes index.
  1. Amusement parks—United States—States—
Directories. I. Norris, Joann, 1947–
II. Title.
GV1853.2.N67   1986   796′.06′873   85-43584

ISBN 0-89950-212-1 (sewn softcover; acid-free natural paper)

Manufactured in the United States of America.

McFarland   Box 611   Jefferson NC 28640

To all of the State Tourist Bureaus, park
owners and employees who help to make so
many fantasies come true. And to our
parents who allowed us to fantasize.

Acknowledgments

Thanks to the Tourist Bureaus in each state, plus all of the publicity people in each park for providing such friendly and helpful information.

Table of Contents

Introduction

If you've visited any amusement or theme parks lately, you've probably noticed many people there sporting T-shirts, totebags, etc., with the names of other parks on them. In our travels, we've talked with many of these people and discovered that a large percentage of them have been to more than two major parks and are planning to visit more in the future. We call these people "amusement park junkies." We also discovered that the only way you find out where many amusement parks are is from other "A.P.J.s" in parks you've visited, or from national advertising by the larger parks. We felt that there had to be smaller (and less expensive) parks out there somewhere that couldn't afford such wide-range publicity, but would nevertheless provide an entertaining day for A.P.J.s and first-timers alike.

This book is a guide to America's amusement and theme parks. Since different types of families seek different types of entertainment from these parks (some go for the shows, some for the sights, some just for the roller coasters), we tried to include as much specific information about each park as we possibly could. The reader can then scan the information to determine if the park offers the types of "thrills" that he or she seeks.

Included at the end of each section is information about other sites of interest with a 100-mile radius.

A Brief History of Amusement Parks in the United States

Man has always sought a thrilling and entertaining adventure for at least part of his leisure time activities. Fairs, feasts and festivals have provided much of this entertainment since recorded history began (or before), offering food, shows, music and even an occasional ride for the ladies and children. In 1893, the Chicago World's Fair became a milestone in amusement history. Exhibited there was a giant 250-foot wheel with thirty glass cabs suspended from its girders. Each cab held sixty people. This huge rotating wheel, invented by G.W. Ferris, was destined to become a regular feature at fairs, carnivals and amusement parks, thus opening up "rides" for the whole family to enjoy. People quickly learned to love and trust mechanical rides as more and more inventors took the lead from Ferris.

The love of fairs and festivals continued, but people began to demand a cleaner, more respectable-looking environment where they could have a good time but not put their lives, or their wallets, in jeopardy. Several organizations were formed with this goal in mind. In 1912, the Carnival Managers' Association of America was formed. Around the same time, the Rice & Dear Floating City Shows created a complete carnival on 24 mammoth barges which they floated from town to town. The carnival included shows, games and rides, in a clean, closely contained area.

In March of 1917, the National Outdoor Showmen's Association (NOSA) was formed. Probably the most important outdoor showmen's association formed up to that time, its top priority was to wipe out "privilege cars" in carnivals. A privilege car was a car, wagon, truck or trailer which was often leased to crooked gamblers who ran rigged games of chance. Sam Gumpertz, NOSA's first vice-president, succeeded moderately in reducing these traps. Other organizations have continued this trend, but in the long run, it is what the people want and can afford that influences the amusement park industry the most.

World's Fairs have proven to be a hit (until recently), and have been located around the world to enable a great range of people to participate in the fair experience. Permanently located amusement parks, however, have had their ups and downs. All show business areas, both in- and out-of-doors, experienced hardships during the Great Depression of the 1930s. Amusement parks were hit hard, but county and state fairs did well, proving that people still wanted a thrill, but had to seek a little less expensive one closer to home.

The mid- to late-1930s saw a resurgence of outdoor entertainment. In 1939, both the New York World's Fair and the Golden Gate Exposition in San Francisco opened for business and proved to be the most ambitious and successful fairs of all time. The fever for outdoor entertainment spread until another disaster, in the form of a 1938 railroad strike, caused some outdoor amusement companies to fold. Some companies decided that a merger would help keep them alive. Rubin & Cherry, Beckman-Gerety and Royal America, all large companies, merged at this time to form the Amusement Corporation of America. Mergers of this type led to larger corporations and larger plans. Amusement parks began springing up around the nation.

The theme park concept was launched in 1955 by "Mr. Showmanship," Walt Disney, inspired by his many visits to European outdoor entertainment areas. Disney created a park with five distinct theme areas — Main Street, U.S.A.; Adventureland; Frontierland; Tomorrowland; and Fantasyland — each with its own rides, shows, restaurants and other attractions, plus life-size Disney characters roaming about. The park was an unbelievable success. Disney succeeded in creating a place where parents could take their children and all of them could have fun. As Walt Disney himself said:

> Disneyland isn't designed just for children. When does a person stop being a child? Can you say that a child is ever entirely eliminated from an adult? I believe that the right kind of entertainment can appeal to all persons, young or old. I want Disneyland to be a place where parents can bring their children — or come by themselves and still have a good time.[1]

---

[1] Quoted by Bob Thomas in *Walt Disney: An American Original* (New York: Simon and Schuster, 1976), 11.

In a commencement speech at the Harvard School of Design in 1963, the noted designer James Rouse stated that Disneyland "took an area of activity—the amusement park—and lifted it to a standard so high in its performance, in its respect for people, that it really became a brand new thing."[2]

In typical Disney fashion, another park was opened in 1972 in Lake Buena Vista, Florida, near Orlando. "Walt Disney World" covers forty-three square miles and consists of the Magic Kingdom theme park (similar to Disneyland), as well as condominiums, hotels, restaurants, shopping centers, campgrounds and golf courses. Stretching the amusement park concept even further, E.P.C.O.T. (Environmental Prototype Community of Tomorrow) Center opened near Disneyworld in 1982. One might best describe E.P.C.O.T. as a gigantic museum-amusement-theme park.

In 1961, Six Flags over Texas was opened about twenty miles from the Dallas–Fort Worth airport on a multiacre site. The Six Flags group eventually opened two more theme parks—Six Flags over Georgia (on 276 acres, about ten minutes from downtown Atlanta) and Six Flags over Mid-America (outside of St. Louis)—and even took over Astroworld in Houston and Great Adventure in Jackson, New Jersey.

The Taft Broadcasting Corporation took over the Hanna-Barbera animated film production company and decided to use the Hanna-Barbera characters in theme parks around the nation. They eventually developed Kings Island near Cincinnati, Ohio, Kings Dominion near Richmond, Virginia, and Carowinds (acquired from another company) in Charlotte, North Carolina. (Carowinds actually sits on the North Carolina–South Carolina border and is publicized by the tourist bureaus in both states.)

Anheuser-Busch developed two theme parks near their main breweries: The Dark Continent in Tampa, Florida, and The Old Country in Williamsburg, Virginia.

The Marriott Corporation opened its first theme park on May 29, 1976. Located in Gurnee, Illinois, near Chicago and Milwaukee, the Great America theme park boasts five main theme areas and uses Warner Brothers characters throughout the park. A second park was soon opened near San Francisco, and a third one is planned near Washington, D.C.

Disney, Six Flags, Taft, Marriott and Anheuser-Busch, each with more than one park in its system, are considered the "Big Five" of the

---

[2] Ibid., 311.

theme park industry. Other parks around the nation, though owned by so-called independents with only one park in the system, still record more than 2,000,000 people per year. These include Knott's Berry Farm in Buena Park, California; Magic Mountain in Valencia, California; Opryland in Nashville, Tennessee; and Cedar Point in Sandusky, Ohio. Parks boasting over 1,000,000 in yearly attendance include Hersheypark in Hershey, Pennsylvania, and Circus World in Haines City, Florida, near Orlando.

More and more amusement parks (not necessarily theme parks) are opening each year. In 1977 there were about forty large amusement parks around the nation. By the fall of 1983, we found that there were more than 150 amusement parks operating on both large and small scales. Many of these smaller parks, such as Dutch Wonderland in Lancaster, Pennsylvania, have been in business for many years, but tend to cater more to local clientele and families with smaller children. These parks offer an enjoyable, exciting, unhurried outing, as most of them can be totally covered in one short day.

Many amusement parks in the northern states have very seasonal business, with facilities being closed for up to nine months of the year. Kings Island Amusement Park in Cincinnati, Ohio, was the first seasonal park to try opening during at least part of the off-season. In 1982, 1983 and 1984, the park opened for about four weeks between Thanksgiving and New Year's. Admission is considerably lower (about one-fourth the regular price) during this "Winterfest" season, which offers a gigantic Christmas lights display, ice skating, buggy rides, hayrides, an original live musical production, street entertainment, carousel rides, a boat ride through an enclosed winter wonderland, and food from many restaurants and shops.

Carowinds, in Charlotte, North Carolina, also opened for Winterfest in 1983. Approximately one-third of the park was opened and decorated for the Christmas season, with activities similar to those at Kings Island, but, of course, adapted to the unique qualities of Carowinds. The park did not open for Winterfest in 1984.

During 1984, many parks, large and small, were working to improve their establishment. Many smaller or older parks were adding decorative landscaping, and most parks were planning to add at least one main attraction (a major ride, garden or live entertainment seemed to be the main goals).

With an increasing amount of leisure time to fill, Americans today are searching for ways to make that time more interesting, even in cold weather. More and more people are choosing to spend time at amusement parks, where they can escape reality and have a thrill.

A Word About
Park Information

As the amusement park industry is in a constant state of change, we suggest that you correspond beforehand with the park(s) you intend to visit. The following pages list the parks by state, giving the addresses and phone numbers (where possible) to which you should address your inquiries. The information you will receive will most likely tell you of major improvements in the park in the past year (or, heaven forbid, that the park is no longer in operation!). Such information, along with this guide, will help you plan an enjoyable experience for you and your family or friends.

Most prices reflect the 1984 season, unless otherwise noted. Please be aware that some prices have risen since then.

Park Information

WaterWorld
Dothan, Alabama

WaterWorld is the "Aquatic Center" of Westgate Park on the west side of Dothan, Alabama. The park is owned and operated by the city of Dothan. Besides WaterWorld, Westgate Park offers tennis courts, racquetball courts, ping-pong tables, a basketball gym, an indoor pool, a weightlifting room, saunas and whirlpools.

WaterWorld itself offers four main water attractions: The Wave Pool; a 400-ft. "Thrill Hill" which offers three different water flumes (for those forty-two inches or taller); and Bumper Boats which are exclusively for three- to nine-year-olds. One concession stand, a picnic area, and a bathhouse are also included in the fifteen-acre park.

Season: Weekends in May; daily from end of May through end of August; open Labor Day (last day).

Best day to attend: Any day.

Hours: 10 a.m.–7 p.m. Mon/Wed/Fri/Sat; 10 a.m.–9 p.m. Tues/Thurs; noon–7 p.m. Sun.

Tickets: Adults, $3.50; children 3–12 years, $2.00; senior citizens (55 and older), $1.00. Half-price after 5 p.m. on Tues/Thurs.

Other Conveniences and Attractions: Picnic facilities, locker and basket rentals (25¢), lost and found, first-aid center, resting benches through the park, raft rental ($2), provisions made for the handicapped, free parking with 250 spaces available, Master Card and Visa accepted.

7

Other sites of interest within fifty miles of the park include the Boll Weevil Monument and the U.S. Army Aviation Museum.

For further information write Waterworld, Westgate Park, Dothan AL 36303, or call (205) 793-0297.

Disneyland
Anaheim, California

Disneyland in California and Disney World in Florida are probably the two most popular of all amusement and theme parks. Opened in 1955, Disneyland consists of five main theme areas with rides, amusements, restaurants and shops, all built around the theme of that particular area. A brief description here cannot do justice to the park, as there is little in the way of family entertainment that Disneyland does not offer.

Season: Year-round.

Hours: Vary according to season, special holidays, etc. Be sure to write to the park before visiting.

Tickets: All day for one admission price. One-day pass, adults $23/children (3–12) $19; Two-day passes and Three-day passes are also available at a lower price. Senior Fun Days offered on Thurs/Fri.

Other Conveniences and Attractions: Arcades, craftsmen at work, parades, street shows, garden walks, camping in and near the park, pet care, picnic area outside park gates, baby center with all baby care items available (not baby-sitting), banking services, guide service available, camera rentals, locker rentals, wheelchairs and strollers, provisions made for handicapped, raincoats and sweatshirts for sale, lost and found, lost parents and first aid center, resting benches throughout park, shooting galleries, break-down service in parking lot, fireworks (occasionally), transportation from parking lot to park, transportation within the park, ample parking — at cost. American Express cards accepted.

Other sites of interest within a few miles of the park include Universal Studio Tours, Knott's Berry Farm, and more.

For further information write Disneyland, Guest Relations, P.O. Box 3232, Anaheim CA 92803, or call (714) 533-4456.

Great America
Santa Clara, California

Located just forty-five minutes south of San Francisco, this 100-acre theme park is northern California's largest amusement park/entertainment center. It opened in 1976 and is owned by the city of Santa Clara and operated by Kings Entertainment Company.

This beautifully landscaped and creatively designed park offers six main theme areas: Carousel Plaza, Hometown Square, County Fair, Yukon Territory, Yankee Harbor, and Orleans Place. The Fort Fun play area, located in Yukon Territory, is designed especially for the younger set. Each theme area offers rides (more than ten major rides in all, plus Kiddie rides in Fort Fun), shops unique to the area, restaurants (twenty in all), photo-posing areas and more.

Great America plans to add at least one major attraction each year, with 1986 bringing "The Grizzly" roller coaster, an expanded Fort Fun area, and a new 10,000-seat amphitheater, which will offer twelve top-name concert performers during the season. (We suggest that you write ahead for reservations to these performances.)

Great America can claim some unique features, one being the carousel "The Columbia," the "largest and most expensive ever built," which sits at the entrance to the park. The 100-foot-tall, double-decker carousel carries 106 enameled figures turning on brass rods, original oil paintings, baroque scrollwork and other unique items.

Season & Hours: Open 10 a.m. daily during Easter week and from May 31 through September 1; open Saturdays and Sundays at 10 a.m. from March 14 through May 31 and from September 2 through October 26. Closing times vary.

Best days to attend: Monday or Tuesday.

Tickets: All day for $13.95; senior citizens 55 and older, $8.50;

children 3 and under, free. Season passes and group rates (25 or more) are also available.

Other Conveniences and Attractions: Parades, street shows, picnic facilities, camera rentals, locker rentals, wheelchairs and strollers, provisions made for handicapped, raincoats and sweatshirts for sale within the park, lost and found, lost parents, first aid center, resting benches throughout the park, free maps of park, transportation from parking lot to park and transportaion within the park, parking spaces available at a cost of $3, fireworks on July 4, most major credit cards accepted.

Other sites of interest within 50 miles include San Francisco sites, beaches and much more.

For further information write Great America, P.O. Box 1776, Santa Clara CA 95052 or call (408) 988-1776.

Knott's Berry Farm
Buena Park, California

This 150-acre park is the oldest theme amusement park in the nation. It is also ranked as the largest independent park, with five main theme areas. Located thirty miles east of downtown Los Angeles and six miles north of Disneyland, the park boasts of gate attendance figures second only to the two Disney parks.

The park celebrated its Sixtieth Anniversary Diamond Jubilee in 1980, having grown from a tiny berry stand in 1920 to the huge entertainment/amusement park that it is now, with 165 rides and attractions. Plans for a large expansion are currently in progress; Phase I was recently completed with the addition of a new theme area which includes thirty new rides and attractions. Landscaping is an integral part of the park, with many trees and covered waiting areas providing shelter from the hot California sun.

Three theaters provide live entertainment daily, with headliner entertainers performing regularly (about twelve shows per season). Six restaurants and twenty-three snack concessions provide a large choice of eating pleasures. Over forty shops, including a bakery, giftshops, souvenir shops and specialty shops, provide plenty of shopping, with souvenirs ranging in price from 50¢ to $10 and up. Three craftsmen exhibit their skills each day.

Season: Daily except Christmas; closed Wed/Thurs during winter. Holidays & special events alter hours.

Hours: 9 a.m.–midnight Sun–Fri; 9 a.m.–1 a.m. Saturday; summer hours are shorter.

Tickets: $11.95 for adults (12 & older); $8.95 for children (3–11), senior citizens and handicapped; under 3 are free.

Other Conveniences and Attractions: Arcade (24 games), playground area, petting zoo, parades, street shows, picnic facilities, guide service available, camera rentals, locker rentals, wheelchair and stroller rentals, raincoats and sweatshirts for sale, lost and found, lost parents, first aid center, resting benches throughout the park, free maps of park, transportation from parking lot to park, fireworks show, padded chairs in the theaters, free parking with 20,000 spaces available, major credit cards accepted.

Other sites of interest within thirty miles of the park are many, the closest being Movieland, Disneyland, Marineland, and Magic Mountain.

For further information write Knott's Berry Farm, Buena Park CA 90622, or call (714) 827-1776.

Marineland
Rancho Palos Verdes, California

Marineland, a seventy-one-acre oceanographic park in southern California, is built on a slightly hilly jetty on the Pacific coast. Landscaping is well done, with approximately ten people employed for this task.

Although the park offers no amusement park–type rides, it does offer a unique swim-through experience in its "Baja Reef." All necessary snorkeling equipment is available for rent ($4). Five live shows are presented throughout the park several times each day. These shows feature dolphins, sea lions, killer whales and other exotic marine life. A Petting Pool allows a hands-on experience with dolphins and sea lions. Top-name entertainment is occasionally performing in one of the air-conditioned theaters.

Four restaurants and five snack facilities provide some variety of food choices, and a panoramic view of the Pacific Ocean and Catalina Island. Shopping offers souvenirs ranging in price from 50¢ to $50.

Season: Year-round.

Hours: 10 a.m.–7 p.m. during summer; 10 a.m.–5 p.m. after Labor Day; closed Mon/Tues during winter.

Best day of the week to attend: Weekdays.

Tickets: $9.95 for Adults; $6.95 for Children (3–11); under 3 are free; special rates for senior citizens.

Other Conveniences and Attractions: Arcade (4 games), playground area, wildlife areas, picnic facilities, camera rentals, locker rentals, wheelchairs and strollers, provisions made for handicapped, raincoats and sweatshirts for sale, lost and found, lost parents, first-aid center, resting benches throughout the park, free maps of park, free parking with 3180 spaces available, credit cards accepted.

Other sites of interest within forty miles of the park include Disneyland, Knotts Berry Farm, Queen Mary and the Spruce Goose.

For further information write Marineland, 6610 Palos Verdes Dr. South, Rancho Palos Verdes CA 90274, or call (213) 772-1188.

Santa Cruz Beach Boardwalk
Santa Cruz, California

The Santa Cruz Beach Boardwalk, located on California's central coast, is the West Coast's last remaining seaside amusement park. Built during the gracious Victorian era of plush seaside resorts, the Santa Cruz has survived approximately seventy-five years of economic ups and downs. Recent park improvements included a $10 million renovation of the Coconut Grove (ballroom and conference center) and several new rides.

A traditional amusement park, Santa Cruz Boardwalk offers nineteen major rides and five kiddie rides. The Giant Dipper wooden roller coaster, built in 1924, is recognized by roller coaster enthusiasts as one of the top ten coasters in the world. Renovations and excellent maintenance keep the rides safe and exciting.

The park has more than nineteen restaurants and snack facilities offering a large range of menu and snack choices. The Coconut Grove serves a Sunday champagne brunch in the Sun Room (reservations helpful). Over fifteen shops provide lots of shopping fun, with souvenirs ranging in price from $1 to $20.

Season: Open daily Memorial Day through Labor Day; weekends rest of the year.

Hours: Usually open at 11 a.m.

Tickets: Admission to the boardwalk is free. A variety of ticket plans include paying for each ride and a $9.50 all-day unlimited ride pass, among others.

Other Conveniences and Attractions: Indoor miniature golf, arcade (300 games), picnic facilities, camping within 10 miles, locker rentals, wheelchairs and strollers, provisions made for handicapped, lost and found, lost parents, first aid center, resting benches throughout park, 1,800 parking spaces at a cost of $3–4, MasterCard and Visa accepted.

Other sites of interest: Besides beaches, Santa Cruz offers few other nearby attractions. San Francisco is eighty miles to the north.

For further information write Santa Cruz Beach & Boardwalk, Santa Cruz CA 95060, or call (408) 423-5590.

Santa's Village
Sky Forest, California

Situated in the woods of the San Bernandino Valley National Forest, Santa's Village amusement park is designed especially for families with young children ages two to twelve. Besides the natural landscaping, four people are employed to maintain the park landscaping.

Twelve kiddie rides are available. One restaurant and three snack bars offer some variety of menu and snack choices. One live show is presented in the bench-seat theater, with top-name entertainment performing occasionally. Five shops offer souvenirs ranging in price from $2 to $10.

Season and Hours: 10 a.m.–5 p.m. daily, June 23–Sept 8 and Nov 9–Jan 5 (closed Christmas Day); open weekends and holidays, Jan 7–Feb 28, May 25–June 22, and Sept 9–Nov 9.

Tickets: $3.50 for admission and extra for rides, or all day for one admission price: $6.50 ages 5 and older, $6.00 ages 3 and 4, 2 and under free. Senior citizen discounts available.

Other Conveniences and Attractions: Horseback riding (mid-May through Sept), playground area, petting zoo, wildlife areas, picnic facilities, camping — on premises and within 10 miles, camera rentals, wheelchairs and strollers, provisions made for handicapped, raincoats and sweatshirts for sale, lost and found, lost parents, first aid center, resting benches throughout the park, free map of park, free parking, most major credit cards accepted.

Other sites of interest within five miles of the park include Lake Arrowhead, Snow Valley, Ice Castles, Fun Company and Arrowhead Ocean.

For further information write Santa's Village, Sky Forest CA 92385.

Sea World
San Diego, California

Sea World in San Diego is one of three marine zoological parks in the nation operated through Sea World Enterprises, Inc. (Harcourt Brace Jovanovich, Inc.). The other parks are located in Cleveland, Ohio, and Orlando, Florida. Situated on the south shore of Mission Bay in southern California, the beautifully landscaped park was founded in 1964 with the idea of combining a quality family entertainment area with an educational presentation of marine life. The park covers a total of 110 acres of a flat terrain with many trees and covered, if not enclosed, exhibits and show areas.

Five shows, thirty educational exhibits, three rides and four aquariums make up the entertainment schedule. Killer whales, dolphins, seals and others, pearl-divers, and a water fantasy display make up the shows. Occasionally top-name entertainers perform, usually during the summer. The rides consist of the PSA Skytower, the Atlantis Skyride and the Sea World Hydrofoils. Seven gift shops and eleven souvenir concessions supply a wide range of shopping pleasures, with actual souvenirs ranging in price from 80¢ to $10. Seven restaurants and thirty snack facilities provide a large range of menu and snack choices, with over 600 people employed in these areas alone.

Season and Hours: Daily 9 a.m.–5 p.m. or 9 a.m.–7:30 p.m. (summer).

Best days to attend: Weekdays.

Tickets: All day for one admission price: Adults, $12.95, children (3–11) and seniors, $9.95, under 3 free.

Other Conveniences and Attractions: Glassblowers, playground area, petting zoo (pool), garden walks, wildlife areas, picnic facilities, camping nearby, guide service available, camera rentals, locker rentals, wheelchairs and strollers, provisions made for handicapped, raincoats and sweatshirts for sale, lost and found, first aid center, resting benches throughout the park, free maps of park, free parking for 7,000 vehicles, transportation from Sea World to the Atlantis Restaurant is available, most major credit cards accepted.

Other sites of interest within ten miles of the park include the Maritime Museum, San Diego Zoo, Old Town State Park, Balboa Park & Museum and Cabrillo State Park.

For further information write Sea World, 1720 South Shores Blvd., San Diego CA 92109, or call (714) 222-6363.

Six Flags Magic Mountain
Valencia, California

Six Flags Magic Mountain is one of the newest of the Six Flags chain of large (this one is 260 acres — 104 in the park proper) family theme parks. The park is located in the northwest section of Los Angeles County, where the weather encourages the growth of more than 11,000 trees and thousands of flowers and blossoming vines. An arboretum exhibits exotic flowers and plants year-round.

The park offers thirty-five major rides and sixteen kiddie rides of all types, including visual, Coney Island–type, water rides and live animal rides. At least one major attraction is added each year. Seven major shows are performed daily, along with the many street shows which wander through the park. Headliner entertainment performs occasionally. Ten restaurants and fifteen snack facilities provide a wide range of food choices, while ten shops offer plenty of shopping.

Season: Summer, daily 10 a.m.–? (hours vary); weekends the rest of the year.

Best days to attend: Weekdays.

Tickets: All day for one admission price: Adults, $13.95, children under 48″ in height, $6.95.

Other Conveniences and Attractions: Three arcades, several craftsmen at work, playground area, "Children's World" play area, petting zoo, parades, street shows, garden walks, wildlife areas, picnic facilities, camping within 10 miles, pet care, guide service available, camera rentals, locker rentals, wheelchairs and strollers, provisions made for the handicapped, raincoats and sweatshirts for sale, lost and found, lost parents, first aid center, resting benches throughout the park, free maps of park, transportation from parking lot to park provided, transportation within the park, covered waiting areas, ample parking spaces at a cost of $2, break-down service in parking lot, fireworks provided, air-conditioned theaters (bench seats), most major credit cards accepted.

Other sites of interest located within 100 miles of the park include Disneyland, Universal Studios, Knott's Berry Farm, Marineland and NBC Studios.

For further information write Six Flags Magic Mountain, Valencia CA 91355, or call (805) 255-4100 or (818) 992-0884.

Quassy Amusement Park
Middlebury, Connecticut

Quassy is a small family amusement park sitting on twenty tree-covered acres in east central Connecticut. Located on crystal clear Lake Quassapaug, the park offers a white sand beach for freshwater swimming, along with the amusement rides.

The park opened in 1908 and now boasts of featuring one of the "oldest and grandest carousels in the country" (brochure), along with nineteen other major rides and nine kiddie rides. Picnicking and family fun have always been among the park's major attractions. Live shows are performed on weekends only. One major restaurant and two snack facilities offer a medium variety of choices for meals and snacks. These facilities are centrally located.

Season: Memorial Day through Labor Day.

Hours: Picnic area opens at 7 a.m., Beach at 10 a.m., Rides at 1 p.m.

Best day to attend: Tuesday.

Tickets: All day for one admission price: adults, $6.50; children under 8, $5.00; or you pay no admission price, but 25¢ per ticket, with rides taking 2, 3, or 4 tickets.

Other Conveniences and Attractions: Arcade ("New England's largest"—150 games), playground area, petting zoo, picnic facilities, camping within 10 miles, locker rentals, raincoats and sweatshirts for sale, lost and found, lost parents, first aid center, resting benches throughout the park, 1 restroom, break-down service available, MasterCard and Visa accepted.

Other sites of interest located within fifteen miles of the park include Holy Land, U.S.A., and Mattatuck Museum.

For further information write Quassy Amusement Park, Rt. 64, Middlebury CT 06762, or call (203) 758-2913.

Funland Amusement Park
Rehoboth Beach Boardwalk
Rehoboth Beach, Delaware

Located in east central Delaware, Funland Amusement Park is situated on the Rehoboth Beach Boardwalk. The small park is mainly an added attraction to the beach area, offering approximately eight major rides and eight kiddie rides.

Season: Memorial Day through Labor Day.

Hours: Open at 1 p.m.

Best day to attend: Mid-week.

Tickets: 10¢ to 70¢ per ride.

Other Conveniences and Attractions: Arcade, wheelchairs and strollers, raincoats and sweatshirts for sale, resting benches throughout the park.

Other sites of interest nearby include the Delaware Seashore State Park.

For further information write General Manager, Rehoboth Beach Boardwalk, Rehoboth Beach DE 19971.

Adventure Island
Tampa, Florida

Located on the west central coast of Florida, Adventure Island is a thirteen-acre outdoor water park offering five theme areas of water fun, including five water slides, a wave pool, a giant speed slide, swimming pool, sand beaches and diving area. The slightly hilly terrain provides some shade trees, and the park provides some covered waiting areas to help protect the patrons from the hot Florida sun.

snack concessions offer a large range of meal and snack choices all over the park. More than twenty shops within the park provide a wide range of souvenirs ranging in price from 50¢ to $2,500.

Season and Hours: Daily, 9:30 a.m.–6 p.m., except summer and selected holidays, when hours are extended.

Best day to attend: Sunday.

Tickets: $13.50 for ages 3 and older; 2 and under are free.

Other Conveniences and Attractions: Craftsmen at work (2–3), playground area, petting zoo, street shows, garden walks, wildlife areas, brewery tours available, picnic facilities, camping within 10 miles, pet care, camera rentals, locker rentals, wheelchairs and strollers, provisions made for handicapped, raincoats and sweatshirts for sale, lost and found, lost parents, first aid center, resting benches throughout the park, free maps of park, 12 large restrooms, transportation from parking lot to park, transportation within the park, 3,940 parking spaces provided at a cost of $1, major credit cards accepted.

Other sites of interest within ninety miles include Adventure Island (next door—summers only), Disney World, E.P.C.O.T. Center, Sea World, Circus World, Ybor City (nearby), beaches and more.

For further information write Busch Gardens–The Dark Continent, Tampa FL 33612, or call (813) 971-8282 or (813) 977-6606.

Circus World
Orlando, Florida

Circus World, located in central Florida, is a 110-acre amusement park built around the Barnum & Bailey Circus theme. The park boasts over 100 rides, shows and attractions. Top-name entertainment performs continually. Besides the Roaring Tiger (the South's longest and fastest roller coaster), eight other major amusement-type rides and six kiddie rides are offered. The main emphasis of the park, however, remains on the numerous circus experiences available.

Many shops within the park offer souvenirs ranging in price from 10¢ to $1,000. Two major restaurants provide some meal choices, while numerous snack facilities offer a large range of snacks.

Season: 365 days a year.

Hours: 9 a.m.–6 p.m.

Tickets: All day for one admission price: Ages 12 and older, $12.95; ages 3–11, $10.95; 2 and under, free; senior citizens discount available.

Other Conveniences and Attractions: Arcade, craftsmen at work, playground area, petting zoo, parades, garden walks, wildlife areas, picnic facilities, camping within 10 miles, pet care, guide service available, camera rentals, wheelchairs and strollers, provisions made for the handicapped, raincoats and sweatshirts for sale, lost and found, first aid center, resting benches throughout the park, free maps of park, covered waiting areas, break-down service available, American Express and MasterCard accepted.

Other sites of interest within five miles of the park include Disney World, Sea World, Lazer World and more. Within ninety miles are Busch Gardens, Adventure Island, Florida beaches and much more.

For further information write Circus World of Florida, P.O. Box 800, Orlando FL 32802, or call (305) 422-0643 or (813) 424-2421.

Cypress Gardens
Cypress Gardens, Florida

Built on a swamp in 1931, Cypress Gardens has become a unique amusement park whose main emphasis is not on rides, but on visual entertainment. Located on 223 slightly hilly acres, the park offers four theme areas featuring magnificent botanical gardens, natural wildlife habitats, live shows, a three-story 180° thrill film, an antebellum Southern village (featuring belles in hoop-skirted dresses), four kiddie rides and the fabulous Water Ski Revue, which has earned for Cypress Gardens the title of "Water Ski Capital of the World." Added in 1983 was the Kodak Island in the Sky, a manmade "island" which slowly carries passengers 200 feet into the air, gently revolving to give each passenger a magnificent view of Lake Eloise and the surrounding countryside.

Three restaurants and numerous concessions provide a large (and delicious) range of meal and snack choices, while twenty-seven shops provide ample shopping opportunities. Souvenir prices range from 50¢ to $20. An unusual lunch experience is offered (based on demand) in the luncheon lake cruise – reservations required.

Season: 365 days a year.

Hours: 8 a.m. till sundown.

Tickets: All day for one admission price: adults, $10.50; children (ages 6-12), $7.00; 5 and under, free.

Other Conveniences and Attractions: Petting zoo, street shows, camping on premises and within 10 miles (reservations required), pet care, camera rentals, locker rentals, wheelchairs and strollers, provisions made for handicapped, raincoats and sweatshirts for sale, lost and found, lost parents, first aid center, resting benches throughout the park, free maps of park, 8 restrooms, transportation from parking lot to park, free parking for 4,000 vehicles, major credit cards accepted.

Other sites of interest within fifty miles include Disney World, Circus World, Busch Gardens, Church Street Station, Florida beaches and more.

For further information write Cypress Gardens, P.O. Box 1, Cypress Gardens FL 33880, or call (813) 324-2111.

E.P.C.O.T. Center
Buena Vista, Florida

A unique entertainment facility, E.P.C.O.T. Center, one part of the Disney World Complex, offers two unique theme areas: World

Showcase and Future World. World Showcase is reminiscent of a World's Fair, but enlarged, while Future World tries to relay what the world of the future may look like.

For further information on this large and unique "amusement" center, we suggest you write to the park itself.

The park offers a large variety of unique eating experiences, but we suggest that you make reservations upon entering the park.

Season: All year, but hours vary and are subject to change without notice.

Tickets: All day for one admission price: Adults, $23; children (3-12), $19; 2 and under, free. A number of combination ticket rates are also available.

Other Conveniences and Attractions: Arcades, computer play center, craftsmen at work, playground area, parades (occasionally), street shows, camping on the Disney World complex, other camping within 10 miles, pet care, guide service available, camera rentals, locker rentals, wheelchairs and strollers, provisions made for the handicapped, raincoats and sweatshirts for sale, lost and found, lost parents, first aid center, resting benches throughout the park, water fountains throughout the park, maps of park — free and at cost, covered waiting areas (mostly inside), break-down service, ample parking spaces at a cost of $2, transportation from parking lot to park, transportation within the park, American Express Card accepted.

Other sites of interest located with five miles include Disney World, other Disney World facilities, Church Street Station, Circus World, Lazer World and more.

For further information write Walt Disney World, Dept. FDM, P.O. Box 40, Lake Buena Vista FL 32830, or call (305) 824-4321.

Miami Seaquarium
Miami, Florida

Miami Seaquarium is located in the southern part of Florida, on fifty acres of near-oceanfront property. Although not an amusement park *per se*, the Seaquarium offers a full day of entertaining and educational marine-life shows and exhibits.

Two shops within the park offer souvenirs ranging from $1 to $25. One restaurant provides a small choice of meals; two snack concessions provide a larger choice of snacks. Trees and covered waiting areas provide relief from the sun.

Season: Year-round.

Hours: 9 a.m.–6:30 p.m.

Tickets: Information unavailable. Senior citizens discount available.

Other Conveniences and Attractions: Garden walks, picnic facilities, pet care, camera rentals, locker rentals, wheelchairs and strollers, provisions made for handicapped, raincoats and sweatshirts for sale, lost and found, lost parents, resting benches throughout the park, free maps of park, free parking for 700 vehicles, elevated monorail ride around the park (free), most major credit cards accepted.

Other sites of interest located within twenty miles of the park include Miami nightlife, the Metrozoo, Viscaya, Coral Castle, Florida beaches and more.

For further information write Miami Seaquarium, 4400 Rickenbacker Cswy., Key Biscayne FL 33149, or call (305) 361-5705.

Sea World
Orlando, Florida

Located in central Florida, Sea World of Orlando covers 135 developed acres of slightly hilly terrain. While the majority of the park is level, several show stadiums are built such that a short uphill walk is necessary to reach them. We suggest that you arrive in plenty of time before each show (at least ten minutes). Shaded rest areas and covered stadiums provide a respite from the sun.

Eight shows are presented each day, with top-name entertainment performing occasionally. Both air-conditioned theaters with individual seats and outdoor theaters with bench seats are used. Many souvenirs can be purchased in the thirteen shops within the park. Souvenirs range in price from $1–up. Six restaurants and eight to twenty snack facilities (including drink carts) provide a wide range of eating and snacking pleasures.

Season: Year-round.

Hours: 9 a.m.–7 p.m. (extended hours in summer).

Best day to attend: Monday or Friday.

Tickets: Adults, $12.95; children (3–11), $10.95; 2 and under, free; senior citizens discount available.

Other Conveniences and Attractions: Live animal rides, 6 craftsmen at work, arcade (79 games), playground area, petting zoo, garden walks, picnic facilities, camping within 10 miles, pet care, guide service available, camera rentals, locker rentals, wheelchairs and strollers, provisions made for handicapped, raincoats and sweatshirts for sale, lost and found, lost parents, first aid center, resting benches throughout the park, free maps of park, 10 sets of restrooms, transportation from parking lot to park, 2800 regular free parking spaces, with 1700 auxiliary spaces available, break-down service available, most major credit cards accepted.

Other sites of interest with five miles of the park include Walt Disney World/E.P.C.O.T. Center, Circus World, and more.

For further information write Sea World of Florida, 7007 Sea World Drive, Orlando FL 32802, or call (305) 351-0021, or toll-free 1-800-432-1178 (inside Florida) or 1-800-327-2420 (outside Florida).

Silver Springs
Silver Springs, Florida

Located in north central Florida, Silver Springs is a 4,500 acre multitheme nature preserve. Operated as a tourist attraction from as early as 1890 by different individuals, the park is now owned and operated by the Leisure Attractions Division of the American Broadcasting Companies. The major attractions within the park include the Reptile Institute, the famous Glass-Bottom Boats, Jungle Cruise, Deer Park and the Antique Car Collection.

Season: Year-round.

Hours: 9 a.m.–5 p.m.

Tickets: Adults, $8.95; children (3–11), $6.75; 2 and under, free.

Other Conveniences and Attractions: Two water rides, wildlife areas, garden walks, camping within 10 miles, pet care, guide service available, wheelchairs and strollers, provisions made for handicapped, 11 shops within the park, 2 restaurants and numerous snack facilities, free parking, most major credit cards accepted.

Other sites of interest within a few miles of the park include Wild Waters (next door) and Florida beaches.

For further information write Silver Springs Public Relatiosn Director, Silver Springs FL 32688, or call (904) 236-2121.

Walt Disney World –
Magic Kingdom
Buena Vista, Florida

The second of the Disney entertainment complexes, Disney World's Magic Kingdom opened in 1972 to offer the same quality of family amusement theme park entertainment as the original Disneyland in California. The Magic Kingdom is one part of the large 28,000 acre supercomplex which also includes E.P.C.O.T. Center, a huge camping complex, resort hotels, River Country (water fun park), Discovery Island, Lake Buena Vista shopping area, and more. For more detailed information, we suggest you write to Walt Disney World itself at:

Walt Disney World
Guest Relations
Buena Vista, Florida 32830

Season: Year-round.

Hours: Vary, and are subject to change without notice.

Best day of the week to attend: Friday.

Tickets: All day for one admission price: Adults, $23; children (3–12), $19; 2 and under, free. A number of combination tickets are also available.

Other Conveniences and Attractions: Arcades, parades (electric light parade is a favorite), street shows, garden walks, camping — on premises and within 10 miles, pet care, guide services (ask for more information, as many types of tours are available), camera rentals, locker rentals, wheelchairs and strollers, provisions made for handicapped, raincoats and sweatshirts for sale, lost and found, lost parents, first aid center, resting benches throughout the park, maps of park — free and at cost, transportation from parking lot to park, transportation within the park, trees and some covered waiting areas, over 7 restaurants and many small snack stands, ample parking at a cost of $2, break-down service available, at least 4 live shows provided several times daily, with top-name entertainment performing occasionally, fireworks provided often, American Express cards accepted.

Other sites of interest within twenty miles of the park include the other areas of the Walt Disney World complex, Sea World, Circus World, Church Street Station and much more.

For further information write Walt Disney World, Dept. FDM, P.O. Box 40, Lake Buena Vista FL, or call (305) 824-4321.

Weeki Wachee Springs
Weeki Wachee, Florida

Located approximately forty-five miles north of Tampa on the west central coast of Florida, this 545-acre multitheme park is owned and operated by the Leisure Attractions Division of the American Broadcasting Companies, Inc. The main attractions of the park include the famous underwater mermaid show, birds of prey and exotic bird shows, wilderness river cruise, pelican orphanage and tropical rain forest. The shows change periodically, as many injured animals are brought to the park, nursed back to health, and then exhibited for a short time before being released into the wild.

Weeki Wachee, although technically a spring, is actually the surfacing point of a large underground river, the bottom of which has still not been located. The constant 72.4° temperature of the water made it a popular swimming and picnicking area as early as the 1900s. The first underwater mermaid show was presented on October 13, 1947, and operated on a small scale until the park was purchased in 1959 by the American Broadcasting Companies. Several additions have been made since that time, although the park remains a visual entertainment center rather than a formal amusement park.

Two restaurants and three snack facilities offer a small choice of inexpensive meals and snacks. Gift shops at the main entrance and on the main walkway offer a small range of souvenir choices.

Season: Year-round.

Hours: 9 a.m.–6 p.m.

Tickets: All day for one admission price: Adults, $6.95; children, $4.75; under 3, free.

Other Conveniences and Attractions: Playground area, petting zoo, garden walks, wildlife areas (besides the shows), camping within 10 miles, pet care, camera rentals, wheelchairs and strollers, provisions made for handicapped, raincoats and sweatshirts for sale, lost and found, lost parents, first aid center, resting benches throughout the park, free maps of the park, free parking available, theaters of all types, most major credit cards accepted.

Other sites of interest within forty-five miles include Buccaneer Bay (adjacent water park), beaches, Busch Gardens and more.

For further information write Weeki-Wachee Springs, U.S. 19 South, Box 97, Weeki Wachee FL 33512, or call (904) 596-2062.

Wild Waters
Silver Springs, Florida

This six-acre water recreation park opened in 1978 next door to Silver Springs park. It is owned and operated by the Leisure Attractions Division of the American Broadcasting Companies, Inc. Many additions have been made to the original park. Its major attractions now include a 450,000-gallon wave pool, eight water slides, a Water Bonanza play area for children, a nine-hole miniature golf course, and a game room.

Season: Daily, March 24–Sept 9

Hours: 10 a.m.–5 p.m.; extended hours to 8 p.m. June 10–Aug 31. Hours subject to change.

Tickets: All day for one admission price: Adults, $6.50; children (3–11), $5.50; 2 and under, free; special rates after 4 p.m. Wild Water/Silver Springs combination ticket is also available at a considerable savings.

Other Conveniences and Attractions: Arcade, picnic facilities, camping within 10 miles, pet care, locker rentals, bathhouse, lost and found, first aid center, resting benches throughout the park, 1 gift shop, 3 food concessions, free parking, major credit cards accepted.

Other sites of interest within ten miles include Silver Springs (next door).

For further information write Wild Waters, Silver Springs, FL 32688.

Six Flags over Georgia
Atlanta, Georgia

Situated in a thickly wooded area outside of Atlanta, this park is the second of the Six Flags chain. The Six Flags reputation for quality is evident throughout the park.

The park offers over thirty major rides and nearly twenty kiddie rides of all types, including visual, Coney Island-type, log flumes, and live animal rides. At least one major attraction is added each year. Several shows are performed daily in the various theaters. Many restaurants and snack facilities provide a large range of meal and snack choices.

Seasons, Hours, Tickets: Information unavailable.

Other Conveniences and Attractions: Arcade, craftsmen at work, playground area, petting zoo, street shows, garden walks, wildlife areas, picnic facilities, pet care, guide service available, camera rentals, locker rentals, wheelchairs and strollers, provisions made for the handicapped, raincoats and sweatshirts for sale, lost and found, lost parents, first aid center, resting benches throughout the park, maps of park — free and at cost, transportation from parking lot to park provided, transportation within the park, covered waiting areas, ample parking spaces, at a cost, break-down service in parking lot, air-conditioned theaters, occasional fireworks provided, most major credit cards accepted.

Other sites of interest located within thirty miles of the park include Stone Mountain, Atlanta nightlife, and White Water Park.

For further information write Six Flags over Georgia, Atlanta GA 30304, or call toll-free 1-800-282-0456 (inside Georgia) or 1-800-241-0802 (outside Georgia).

White Water
Atlanta, Georgia

A family outdoor water-fun park.

For further information, see White Water, Grand Prairie, Texas or write White Water Park, Atlanta GA 30304.

Paradise Park
Honolulu, Hawaii

Paradise Park, located four and one-half miles from Waikiki, is a fifteen-acre park that features not only a relaxing atmosphere, but also a glimpse of Hawaii's history. The park, situated in Manoa Valley, is one of the "most beautiful and historically significant spots in Hawaiian history" (1984 brochure). In this area Kamehameha the Great prepared for the battle that helped him to conquer and unite the Hawaiian Islands. Queen Koahumanu lived here also.

The famous tropical park offers over fifteen acres of jungle trails, exhibits, and shows, which feature exotic birds, dancing waters, comical ducks, Hawaiian arts and crafts, and guided tours.

Five shops provide shopping for souvenirs ranging in price from $1-20. One main restaurant and three snack facilities provide a medium range of meal and snack choices.

Season and Hours: Daily 9:30 a.m.–5:00 p.m.

Tickets: All day for one admission price: Adults, $7.50; juniors (13-17), $6.50; children (4-12), $3.75; 3 and under, free. Admission/lunch packages also available.

Other Conveniences and Attractions: Craftsmen at work, guide service available, camera rentals, wheelchairs and strollers, provisions made for handicapped, raincoats and sweatshirts for sale, lost and found, lost parents, first aid center, resting benches throughout the park, free maps of park, 4 restrooms, free shuttle buses from hotels in Waikiki, free parking for 100 vehicles, major credits cards accepted.

Other sites of interest within a few miles include the Lyon Arboretum, Bishop Museum and Atherton Halau.

For further information write Paradise Park, Inc., 3737 Manon Rd., Honolulu HI 96822.

Waimea Falls Park
Haleiwa, Hawaii

Although not a traditional amusement park, Waimea Falls Park offers a full day of sightseeing amusements, in a botanical and zoological setting. The park covers 1,800 acres and was the location of a native habitat for several hundred years. The preservation and reconstruction of this historic site is ongoing, and all collections, sites, etc., are carefully labeled for the visitor's enjoyment. Besides the botanical gardens and historic living site, visitors can take in cliff divers, Hawaiian hula dancers, Hawaiian game demonstrations, wildlife feeding and a Burial Temple tour. Shopping and restaurants are also available.

Season and Hours: Daily, 10 a.m.–5:30 p.m.

Best day to attend: Tuesday.

Other Conveniences and Attractions: Picnic facilities, camping on the premises and within 10 miles, pet care, guide service available, camera rentals, wheelchairs, provisions made for handicapped, raincoats and sweatshirts for sale, lost and found, lost parents, first aid center, resting benches throughout the park, free maps of park, transportation within the park provided, free parking is provided for 520 vehicles, most major credit cards accepted.

For further information write Waimea Falls Park, 59-864 Kamehameha Highway, Haleiwa HI 96712.

Lincoln Land Amusement Park
Effingham, Illinois

Lincoln Land Amusement Park, located in central Illinois, is one of the very few amusement parks which is entirely enclosed and air conditioned. One person is employed to maintain the indoor landscaping. Covering three acres, the park includes indoor tennis, an eighteen-hole miniature golf course and a roller skating rink, along with the eleven amusement rides.

The park also offers two to three live shows, with top-name entertainment performing occasionally. One restaurant and three snack facilities offer a medium range of meal and snack choices. Two stores provide shopping, with souvenirs ranging in price from 50¢ to $10.

Season: Winter: Fri/Sat/Sun. Summer: Wed–Sun.

Hours: Opens at noon.

Tickets: No admission price: 50¢ per ride.

Other Conveniences and Attractions: Arcade (60 games), picnic facilities, camping within 10 miles, lost and found, resting benches throughout the park, free parking with 2500 spaces available, breakdown service, fireworks (occasionally).

Other sites of interest within seventy miles include Abraham Lincoln sites and St. Louis, Missouri.

For further information write Lincoln Land Amusement Park, P.O. Box 1079, Effingham IL 62401, or call (217) 342-2924.

Marriott's Great America
Gurnee, Illinois

One of the Marriott Corporation's chain of amusement parks, Great America is located in northeastern Illinois, just forty-five minutes north of Chicago. The park is designed with a circular layout so that visitors will easily be able to see and do everything in an orderly fashion. Most park operations and maintenance are carried out from the central core. The five historical-theme areas are well separated by shrubbery or other visual barriers, and visitors travel from one area to another through a covered bridge. The 200-acre park employs over 120 people specifically for landscaping maintenance, and over 80 people specifically for park maintenance (cleanliness). The many trees and covered waiting areas provide shelter from the summer sun.

One of the first of the Marriott parks to open (in 1976), Great America is an exact replica of each of the others. The original goal of the management was to reach the regional public, rather than the traveling public. Wherever the visitors come from, however, chances are they will note the attention to detail for which the Marriott chain is noted for.

Live musicals, grand illusions, and animal acts make up the many shows, with top-name entertainment occasionally on the billing. Over thirty-nine rides, including the American Eagle (world's largest double racing wooden roller coaster), offer the riding "thrills" most park visitors are seeking. Over twenty-eight shops offer a large range of shopping choices, with souvenirs ranging in price from 25¢ to $30. Forty restaurants and forty-two snack facilities, employing 1200 people, allow the visitor to choose from a large range of eating pleasures.

Season: Weekends, May and Sept; daily, May 23 to Sept 5.

Hours: Opens at 10 a.m.

Best day to attend: Friday.

Tickets: All day for one admission price: Ages 4–54, $12.95; 55 and older, $7.75; 3 and under, free.

Other Conveniences and Attractions: Arcade (16 games), craftsmen at work, parades, street shows, picnic facilities, camping within 10 miles, pet care, camera rentals, locker rentals, wheelchairs and strollers, provisions made for handicapped, raincoats and sweatshirts for sale, lost and found, lost parents, first aid center, resting benches throughout the park, maps of park — free and at cost, transportation from parking lot to park, transportation within the park, covered waiting areas, 10,000 parking spaces at a cost of $3, break-down service, fireworks on the 4th of July, most major credit cards accepted.

Other sites of interest closeby include Chicago attractions and Lake Michigan.

For further information write Marriott's Great America, P.O. Box 1776, Gurnee IL 60031, or call (312) 249-4960.

Santa's Village
Dundee, Illinois

Santa's Village, located in the northwest part of Illinois, is a fifty-five acre amusement center. Although the park is situated on slightly hilly ground, trees and mostly flat ground make the walking cool and comfortable. Amusement-type rides and live animal rides are available for "kids" of all ages.

One main store provides souvenirs at a cost of 5¢ and up. Three restaurants provide a medium range of meal choices, while eight snack concessions offer a larger range of snack choices.

Tickets: All-day admission for $6.50.

Other Conveniences and Attractions: Playground area, petting zoo, picnic facilities, camping within 10 miles, camera rentals, strollers, provisions made for handicapped, raincoats and sweatshirts for sale, lost and found, first aid center, resting benches throughout the park, free parking with 1500 spaces available, MasterCard and Visa accepted.

Other sites of interest nearby include Marriott's Great America and Chicago attractions.

For further information write Santa's Village, Routes 25 & 72, Dundee IL 60118, or call (312) 426-6751.

Indiana Beach
Monticello, Indiana

Indiana Beach, situated on Lake Shafer in north central Indiana, is a combination summer resort and amusement park. All types of overnight accommodations are available. The park itself covers approximately thirty-seven acres, extending along the lake shore for nearly one-half mile. New attractions are added annually. Although trees aren't abundant in the park proper, the landscaping does provide areas where visitors can seek relief from the sun.

Three restaurants, two nightclubs, and thirteen snack facilities offer a wide range of meal and snack choices — not only in food, but in atmosphere as well. The five shops provide souvenirs ranging in price from 25¢ to $8 and up. A ski show is the only show in the actual park site, but the nightclubs offer entertainment several nights per week.

Season: May 18–Sept 3.

Hours: Opens at 9:00 a.m.

Best day to attend: Monday.

Tickets: General admission: 50¢ for ages 7 to 64, others admitted free. Rides priced from 75¢ to $2.50; 6-hour ticket available for some rides: Adults, $6.50; under 7, $3.50.

Other Conveniences and Attractions: Arcade (150 games), craftsman at work, picnic facilities, camping on premises, provisions made for handicapped, sweatshirts for sale, lost and found, lost parents, resting benches throughout the park, 5 restrooms, some covered waiting areas, free parking with 800 spaces available and 125 parking spaces at a cost of $1, fireworks occasionally, swimming and some water rides, most major credit cards accepted.

Other sites of interest located within a few miles include Lake Michigan, Chicago and more.

For further information write Indiana Beach Resort/Amusement Park, 306 Indiana Beach Drive, Monticello IN 47960, or call (219) 583-4141.

Redbrush Park
Seymour, Indiana

Located in south central Indiana, Redbrush Park is a combination miniresort, campground, water park and amusement park. Each area is emphasized and an important part of the complex. Although the park covers 1076 acres, the amusement park section is small, with five main rides and three kiddie rides available. Picnicking, fishing, boating, hiking, and swimming are some of the other amusements available in the rest of the park.

Two shops in the park offer shopping for souvenirs ranging in price from 50¢ to $12. One main restaurant and three snack facilities offer a medium range of meal and snack choices. Although live shows are not a part of the regularly planned schedule, entertainment is sometimes provided for special holidays and events.

Season: Sept and Oct: Fri/Sat/Sun; May 27–Sept 5: daily.

Hours: Opens at 10 a.m.

Best day to attend: Any weekday.

Tickets: General admission: Ages 4–9, $3.50; ages 60 and older, $3.50; ages 10–59, $3.95; under 4, free. Tickets for rides are 30¢ each or 4/$1 (rides require 1 or more tickets). Pay one-price armband: $3.75.

Other Conveniences and Attractions: Arcade (10 games), playground area, petting zoo, picnic facilities, wildlife areas, camping on premises, locker rentals, provisions made for handicapped, raincoats and sweatshirts for sale, first aid center, resting benches throughout the park, free maps of park, transportation within the park, free parking with 1000 spaces available, fireworks (occasionally), major credit cards accepted.

Other sites of interest within a few miles include Wave Tek Park, Lincoln Boyhood Park and Santa Claus Land.

For further information write Redbrush Park, P.O. Box 100, Seymour IN 47274, or call (812) 497-2480.

Santa Claus Land
Santa Claus, Indiana

Located in south central Indiana, this park claims, "The REAL Santa Claus is at Santa Claus Land, has been Santa for 68 years and ever since the park opened in 1946." Situated on forty-five acres of hilly southern Indiana terrain, the park offers plenty of trees, as well as covered waiting areas, to provide shade while waiting to see "Santa."

Aside from the excitement of seeing Santa, the park also has eighteen amusement rides (nine kiddie rides) to offer thrills to the traditional amusement parkgoer. Seven shops within the park offer a large range of "Christmas" shopping, along with other shopping pleasures. Souvenirs range in price from 25¢ to $10. Six restaurants and seven snack facilities offer a medium range of meal and snack choices. Five shows are presented in the park, although top-name entertainment never appears (other than Santa, that is).

Tickets: All day for $6.25.

Best day to attend: Friday.

Other Conveniences and Attractions: Arcade (48 games), 2 craftsmen at work, petting zoo, garden walks, picnic facilities, camping on premises, camping within 10 miles, pet care, wheelchairs and strollers, provisions made for handicapped, raincoats and sweatshirts for sale, lost and found, lost parents, first aid center, resting benches throughout the park, free maps of park, covered waiting areas, free parking with 850 spaces available, MasterCard and Visa accepted.

Other sites of interest nearby include Wave-Tek Water Park, Redbrush Park, and Lincoln Boyhood Park.

For further information write Santa Claus Land, #1 Santa Claus Square, P.O. Box 37, Santa Claus IN 47579, or call (812) 937-4401.

Wave-Tek Water Park
Clarksville, Indiana

Located in southern Indiana, Wave-Tek is a traditional water-fun park. The park sits on one flat acre, with trees and covered waiting areas provided. Two food establishments provide a medium range of meal and snack choices. Other than what is listed below, no further information was available.

Season and Hours: Summer — 11 a.m.–?

Best days to attend: Mon–Thurs.

Tickets: All day for $4.50, plus Water Boggan — $1.75 for 30 minutes. Combination of the two above: $5.50.

Other Conveniences and Attractions: Playground area, garden walks, petting zoo, picnic facilities, camping on premises, camping within 10 miles, locker rentals, provisions made for handicapped, lost and found, first aid center, free parking with 200 spaces available, breakdown service available.

Other sites of interest nearby include the Lincoln Boyhood Park and Santa Claus Land.

For further information write Wave-Tek Water Park, 505 Marriott Drive, Clarksville IN 47130, or call (812) 283-4411.

Beech Bend
Amusement Park & Campgrounds
Bowling Green, Kentucky

One of the oldest amusement centers in the South, Beech Bend was opened in 1888 to provide an inexpensive, fun day for local residents. Camping was the main emphasis then, and is still, with over 6,500 campsites available on a no-reservations-necessary basis. Situated on 354 beautiful acres in southeastern Kentucky, the park offers all sorts of camping experiences, from swimming to fishing to hiking.

Beech Bend is probably one of the most unusual parks around. Aside from the camping area where all of your needs are provided for, the amusement park offers twenty-eight rides, a huge swimming pool in the middle of the amusement park proper, a water slide, a skating rink, paddle boats, miniature golf, and a lake, located right in the middle of the park, on which you can fish without a license. Three shops and several craft concessions provide souvenirs ranging in price from 10¢ to $20. Five restaurants and four snack concessions provide a large range of meal and snack choices. Six shows are provided daily, ranging from musical and stage productions to street bands. Bluegrass, Gospel, Country and Rock'n'Roll are heard, with Grand Ole Opry stars often appearing on stage.

Season: May–Sept.

Hours: Opens 10 a.m. Sat/Sun; noon Mon–Fri.

Best day to attend: Sunday.

Tickets: All day for $6.50.

Other Conveniences and Attractions: Arcade (55 games), playground area, parades, street shows, garden walks, wildlife areas, picnic facilities, camping on premises, guide service available, provisions made for handicapped, raincoats and sweatshirts for sale, lost and found, lost parents, first aid center, resting benches throughout the park, free maps of park, transportation within the park, covered waiting areas, free parking with 3500 spaces available, break-down service, fireworks (occasionally), International Drag Race Track on site, special events each weekend.

Other sites of interest within a few miles of the park include Mammoth Cave and numerous historic sites.

For further information write Beech Bend Amusement Park, Bowling Green KY 42101, or call (502) 781-7634.

Fun Town Amusements
Saco, Maine

Located in the southeastern corner of Maine, Fun Town is a traditional small amusement park. Covering twenty-four acres, the park is beautifully landscaped and manicured, with over ten people employed for these tasks alone. Over seventeen rides (nine kiddie rides) are available, although there are no live shows. One main store in the park provides shopping with souvenirs ranging in price from 50¢ up. Three restaurants and one snack facility provide some meal and snack choices.

Season: Weekends, mid–April through June 10; daily till Labor Day.

Best day to attend: Sunday.

Hours: Opens at 11 a.m.

Tickets: No information available.

Other Conveniences and Attractions: Arcade (90 games), picnic facilities, camping within 10 miles, provisions made for handicapped, raincoats and sweatshirts for sale, lost and found, lost parents, resting benches throughout the park, free parking with 600 spaces available, break-down service.

Other sites of interest within three miles of the park include Portland and Old Orchard Beach.

For further information write Fun Town Amusements, Rt. 1, Portland Rd., Saco ME 04072, or call (207) 284-5139.

Palace Playland Amusements
Old Orchard Beach, Maine

Although it is not an enormous park, Palace Playland lays claim to many unique features: the largest arcade in New England; the largest roller coaster in New England; the longest waterslide in New England; an antique carousel (handcarved in 1906 by the Philadelphia Toboggan Co.); and Maine's only pirate ship ride. Situated on seven miles of beach on Maine's southeastern shore, the park has ocean breezes to keep visitors cool, which is fortunate, as there are no trees or covered waiting areas.

The park offers fifteen rides (five kiddie rides) but no live shows. Ample shopping is available, however, with twelve shops offering souvenirs ranging in price from 40¢ to $150. One restaurant and five snack concessions offer a medium range of meal and snack choices.

Season: No information available.

Best day to attend: Monday.

Tickets: All day for $8.50, or pay no admission price, and 50¢ a ticket (rides take 1 or more tickets).

Other Conveniences and Attractions: Arcade (300+ games), 3 craftsmen at work, guide service available, camping within 10 miles, locker rentals, provisions made for handicapped, raincoats and sweatshirts for sale, lost and found, lost parents, first aid center, resting benches throughout the park, free maps of park, transportation within the park, 100 parking spaces at a cost of $3–$5, break-down service, fireworks (occasionally).

Other sites of interest located within a few miles of the park include Fun Town Amusement Park and the Portland area.

For further information write Palace Playland Amusements, P.O. Box 355, Old Orchard Beach ME 04064, or call (207) 934-2001.

Wild World
Mitchellville, Maryland

Located twenty-five miles from Washington, D.C., and around forty miles from Baltimore, Wild World offers over 230 acres of rides, water rides, shows and attractions. Cleanliness and the beautiful, natural landscaping are readily apparent as over sixty people are employed for those tasks. Many trees and covered waiting areas help protect park visitors from the elements.

Opened in 1982, the park has completed at least one major expansion each year. There are presently eight major rides and nine kiddie rides, plus a wave pool, three water slides and a kiddie water-fun section. Kiddie City, designed especially for children from toddler to preteen, was scheduled to open in 1985.

Five live shows are presented indoors and out, with top-name entertainment performing occasionally. Four shops offer ample shopping with souvenirs ranging in price from 50¢ to $20. Four restaurants and eight snack facilities offer some range of meal and snack choices. Service is very good, with over 300 people employed in the food service area alone.

Season: Weekends in May; daily starting the end of May.

Best days to attend: Monday, Tuesday and Wednesday.

Tickets: All day for one admission price: Adults, $9.95; ages 4–11, $7.95; 3 and under, free.

Other Conveniences and Attractions: Playground area, petting zoo, street shows, garden walks, picnic facilities, camping within 10 miles, pet care, camera rentals, locker rentals, wheelchairs and strollers, provisions made for handicapped, raincoats and sweatshirts for sale, lost and found, lost parents, first aid center, resting benches throughout the park, free maps of park, covered waiting areas, 5000 parking spaces at a cost of $2, fireworks (July only), most major credit cards accepted.

Other sites of interest located nearby include Kings Dominion and Hershey Park (2-hours drive).

For further information write Wild World, Rt. 214, 13710 Central Ave., Mitchellville MD 20716, or call (301) 249-1500.

Mountain Park
Holyoke, Massachusetts

This 260-acre amusement park (100 acres of entertainment area), located in south central Massachusetts, offers the traditional giant midway atmosphere. The area is mountainous, but other than the climb up the incline from the parking lot to the entrance, most of the park is built for comfortable walking. Trees, a few covered waiting areas, and the altitude help to provide relief from the summer sun.

Twenty-eight major rides and fourteen kiddie rides provide a full day of thrills. Live shows are usually presented only during holidays and on Sundays. One main shop and other smaller concessions provide souvenirs ranging in price from 50¢ to $25. Three restaurants and three snack facilities offer a medium range of meal and snack choices.

Season: Daily from Easter to the last Sunday in September.

Hours: Opens at 1 p.m.

Best days to attend: Midweek.

Tickets: All day for $4.50, or pay no admissions price but pay various prices for individual rides.

Other Conveniences and Attractions: Arcade (50 games), 6 craftsmen at work, picnic facilities (beautiful!), camping within 10 miles, camera rentals, provisions made for handicapped, lost and found, lost parents, first aid center, resting benches throughout the park, covered waiting areas, free parking with 3000 spaces available, breakdown service, fireworks (occasionally).

Other sites of interest located within thirty-five miles of the park include Alpine Slide (next door), Riverside Amusement Park, and the Springfield, Massachusetts, attractions.

For further information write Director, Advertising and Group Sales Promotion, Mountain Park, Rt. 5, Holyoke MA 01040, or call (413) 534-5656.

Riverside Park
Agawam, Massachusetts

Riverside Park in south central Massachusetts is a strong blend of old and new. Originally opened in 1840 as a picnic area, the park has undergone many changes in management, each bringing improvements, until today it offers over 100 rides, shows and attractions for people of all ages. The park is undergoing a beautification program, which, if it continues as well as it has been going, will make the park one of the most attractive in the area. Currently, the old and the new parts of the park are markedly different, but the program should change that.

Situated on 164 slightly (but not inconveniently) hilly acres, the park currently offers over thirty-three major rides and seventeen kiddie rides, many of which are new. The Cyclone roller coaster is one of the newest additions. It was rated #1 in the nation by the American Coaster Enthusiasts Organization in 1983. Approximately four different shows are performed several times each day throughout the park. Ten shops provide shopping "entertainment," with souvenirs ranging in price from $1 to $35 and up. Over thirty-five food establishments, employing around 200 people, offer a wide range of meal and snack choices.

Season: Daily, March 31–October 8.

Hours: Opens at 11 a.m.

Best day to attend: Monday or Tuesday.

Tickets: All day for one admission price: Ages 9 and older, $9.95; ages 3–8, $6.95; 2 and under, free.

Other Conveniences and Attractions: Nine craftsmen at work, playground area, petting zoo, parades, street shows, garden walks, picnic facilities, pet care, camera rentals, wheelchairs and strollers, provisions made for handicapped, raincoats and sweatshirts for sale, lost and found, lost parents, first aid center, resting benches throughout the park, maps of park—at cost, transportation from parking lot to park, transportation within the park, covered waiting areas, 8,000 parking spaces at a cost of $1, breakdown service, fireworks occasionally, some credit cards accepted.

Other amusements located within thirty miles include Mountain Park and the Springfield, Massachusetts, attractions.

For further information write Public Relations Manager, Riverside Park, Rt. 159, Agawam MA 01001, or call (413) 786-9300.

Whalom Lake Park
Fitchburg, Massachusetts

Located in north central Massachusetts, Whalom Lake Park celebrated its ninetieth birthday in 1984. This forty-four-acre traditional family amusement center currently offers thirty-seven rides (thirteen are kiddie rides), as well as a ballroom, roller skating rink, miniature golf course, and picnicking and swimming areas. These attractions supply a young family with a full day of both exciting and relaxing amusements.

Two live shows are presented daily. One restaurant offers a small choice of meals, while three snack facilities offer a large range of snacks. Picnicking is a major attraction, with three large, shady areas designed especially for that purpose. Landscaping includes many shade trees, and some covered waiting areas are included.

Season: Easter to Memorial Day: weekends only; Memorial Day to Labor Day: Tues–Sun.

Best day of the week to attend: Tuesday through Friday.

Tickets: All day for $7.00.

Other Conveniences and Attractions: Arcade (50 games), street shows, picnic facilities, camping within 10 miles, locker rentals, wheelchairs and strollers, provisions made for handicapped, raincoats and sweatshirts for sale, lost and found, lost parents, first aid center, resting benches throughout the park, free maps of park, covered waiting areas, free parking with 1400 spaces available, fireworks (occasionally).

Other sites of interest within thirty miles of the park include all the attractions of Boston.

For further information write Whalom Lake Park, Rt. 13, Whalom District, Fitchburg MA 01420, or call (617) 342-3707.

Pleasure Island
Muskegon, Michigan

Pleasure Island is a traditional water park which offers a large picnic area, a food concession stand, video arcade, gift shop, two 280′ slides, a 410′ corkscrew slide, trolley drop, rampage slide, bumper boats, pedal boats, kiddie water slides and water play area, water cannons and an eighteen-hole miniature golf course.

Season: Daily, Memorial Day through Labor Day.

Tickets: All day for one admission price: Adults, $6.75; Children, $5.75; or $2.50 general admission. After 5:30 p.m.: Adults, $4; Children, $3.

Other Conveniences and Attractions: Arcade, picnic facilities, first aid center, bathhouse, free parking.

For further information write Pleasure Island, Muskegon MI.

Six Flags AutoWorld
Flint, Michigan

This unique twenty-two-acre amusement/entertainment complex, located in eastern Michigan, is the first family entertainment center totally based on an automobile theme. It is also the largest indoor theme park in the world, having seven acres completely enclosed, with three interconnecting buildings making up the complex. In this indoor facility are "total involvement rides" with super-animated characters, computerized hands-on educational exhibits, and special effects shows.

The park management recommends that the visitor plan on spending approximately five hours for a visit. Besides the four rides and the nine shows, visitors have access to ten shops, which provide a wide range of souvenirs priced from 25¢ to $100. Four restaurants and twelve snack facilities provide a medium range of meal and snack choices.

Season: Year-round, days vary.

Hours: Vary with the season.

Tickets: All day for one admission price: Adults and children, $8.95; senior citizens, $6.95; 3 and under, free.

Other Conveniences and Attractions: Arcade, 10 craftsmen at work, playground area, street shows, garden walks, picnic facilities, camping within 10 miles, camera rentals, wheelchairs and strollers, provisions made for the handicapped, raincoats and sweatshirts for sale, lost and found, lost parents, first aid center, resting benches throughout the park, maps of park—at cost, transportation from parking lot to park, 2800 parking spaces at a cost of $1, break-down service, MasterCard and Visa accepted.

Other sites of interest within twenty miles of the park include Crossroads Village, Frankenmuth, and the Waterstreet Pavilion.

For further information write Six Flags AutoWorld, P.O. Box 200, Flint MI 48502, or call (313) 233-7000 or (313) 233-5500.

Paul Bunyan Center
Brainerd, Minnesota

Located in central Minnesota, this fifty-five-acre park sits on a flat terrain in "Paul Bunyan Country" and is planned around a lumbering theme. A twenty-six-foot-tall giant lumberjack greets visitors (occasionally by name), smiles, winks and tells tales. Also on exhibit are his pets, Babe the Blue Ox and Sport the Reversible Dog.

Fifteen rides (five kiddie rides), picnic grounds, animal shows and weekend stage shows (during July and August) are the main attractions. Two shops offer a choice of souvenirs ranging in price from 25¢ to several dollars. Three food concessions offer a medium range of meal and snack choices.

Season: Memorial Day to Labor Day

Hours: Opens at 10 a.m.

Best days to attend: Tuesday through Friday.

Tickets: 65¢ admission plus cost for each ride.

Other Conveniences and Attractions: Arcade (40 games), street shows, picnic facilities, camping within 10 miles, strollers, provisions made for handicapped, sweatshirts for sale within the park, lost and found, lost parents, resting benches and covered waiting areas, free parking with 150 spaces available.

Other sites of interest within twenty miles of the park include Lumbertown, U.S.A., Brainerd International Raceway, Deer Forest/Storybook Land and the Paul Bunyan Arboretum.

For further information write Paul Bunyan Center, c/o Brainerd Area Chamber of Commerce, 6th & Washington Streets, Brainerd MN 56401.

Valleyfair
Shakopee, Minnesota

Valleyfair in mideastern Minnesota is a fifty-five-acre amusement park located approximately twenty minutes from downtown Minneapolis–St. Paul. This large entertainment center offers both trees and covered waiting areas as protection from the elements. The landscaping is well done, with over eighteen people employed specifically to handle this task. Over seventy-five people are employed in maintaining park cleanliness.

Over twenty-six rides (six or more kiddie rides) offer entertainment for riding enthusiasts, while other visitors are entertained by shows at the aqua arena, cartoon characters wandering through the park, the 500-seat Imax Theatre, the arcade, games of skill and the waterslide (at extra cost). Over fifteen shops offer souvenirs ranging in price from 25¢ to $200. Three areas of the park provide live entertainment, with approximately nine different groups performing. Top-name entertainment performs four–five times each year. Theaters range in style from outdoor/bench theaters to air-conditioned/individual seat theaters. The four restaurants and approximately fifteen snack concessions provide a medium–large range of meal and snack choices.

Valleyfair is a sister-park to Cedar Point in Sandusky, Ohio.

Season: Daily, mid-May through Labor Day; weekends in September.

Hours: Opens at 10 a.m.

Tickets: All day for $11.50.

Other Conveniences and Attractions: Arcade (25 games), 2 craftsmen at work, playground area, petting zoo, parades, street shows, garden walks, picnic facilities, camping on premises, camping within 10 miles, camera rentals, locker rentals, wheelchairs and strollers, provisions made for handicapped, raincoats and sweatshirts for sale, lost and found, lost parents, first aid center, resting benches throughout the park, maps of park — at cost, transportation within the park, covered waiting areas, free parking with 6000 spaces available, fireworks (July 4), most major credit cards accepted (including Shopper's Charge).

Other sites of interest located within fifteen miles include the Minneapolis–St. Paul area sites. Canadian border is also nearby.

For further information write Valleyfair, One Valleyfair Drive, Shakopee MN 55379, or call (612) 445-7600.

Silver Dollar City
Marvel Cave Park, Missouri

Silver Dollar City sits on forty improved acres of a 2,000-acre park. Although it does not qualify as an "amusement park" *per se*, the park does offer an entertaining day of sightseeing and show-viewing with over fifteen shows of all types given each day.

Besides shows, the park offers more than twenty shops, with souvenirs ranging in price from $1 to $10,000. Eight restaurants and numerous snack concessions provide a large range of meal and snack choices. If you're into things western, you'll love this park.

Tickets: Adults, $13.95, ages 5–11, $9.95; under 5, free.

Other Conveniences and Attractions: 50 craftsmen at work, playground area, petting zoo, parades, street shows, camping within 10 miles, wheelchairs and strollers, provisions made for handicapped, raincoats and sweatshirts for sale, lost and found, lost parents, first aid center, resting benches throughout the park, free maps of park, transportation from parking lot to park, free parking with 5000 spaces available, break-down service, most major credit cards accepted.

Other sites of interest are located within five miles of the park.

For further information write Silver Dollar City, Marvel Cave Park MO 65616.

Six Flags over Mid-America
Eureka, Missouri

Located thirty minutes west of St. Louis, Six Flags over Mid-America sits on 200 acres of foothill terrain. Many trees, along with some covered waiting areas, provide ample shade. Looney Tunes characters stroll daily through the park, providing picture-taking opportunities for parents. More than thirty rides and four kiddie rides are available, including "Colossus — the Giant Wheel," a 180-foot ferris wheel, one of the biggest in the nation.

Fall weekends bring the park's famous "County Fair," which includes country performers, extra craftsmen displaying their trades, special foods, and special events in the arena area. During the rest of the season, four live shows are performed daily, with top-name entertainment periodically on the billing (at no extra cost). Forty-seven concession stands and restaurants offer a wide range of food choices, while forty-two shops offer an equally wide range of souvenir choices, with prices ranging from $.50 to $100.

Season: Weekends, mid-April to late May; daily, May 23 through Labor Day; weekends, Labor Day through first weekend in October.

Best day to attend: Monday.

Tickets (1986): All day for one admission price: Adults, $13.95;

children (3–11), $9.95; senior citizens (55 and older), $8.95. Two-day and season passes are also available at a considerable savings.

Other Conveniences and Attractions: Arcade, 3 craftsmen at work, playground area, street shows, picnic facilities, camping within 10 miles, pet care, camera rentals, locker rentals, wheelchairs and strollers, provisions made for handicapped, raincoats and sweatshirts for sale, lost and found, lost parents, first aid center, resting benches throughout the park, maps of park (at cost), 16 restrooms, transportation from parking lot to park, 5000 parking spaces at a cost of $2, break-down service available, most major credit cards accepted.

Other sites of interest include St. Louis area sites.

For further information write Six Flags over Mid-America, Eureka MO 63025, or call (314) 938-5300.

White Water
Branson, Missouri

A family outdoor water-fun park.

For further information, see White Water, Grand Prairie, Texas, or write White Water Park, Branson MO.

Benson's Animal Park
Hudson, New Hampshire

Located in southeastern New Hampshire, this 70-acre park claims to be "North America's Oldest Animal Park." The zoo contains over 1,000 exotic birds and animals from around the world. Being situated on a slightly hilly and lightly wooded area helps provide a more natural setting for the zoo animals.

While the zoo is the main attraction at Benson's, it is not the only one. Sixteen rides and four kiddie rides, as well as live animal rides, are offered. Five or six live shows are also presented each day. Three shops provide souvenir shopping. Two restaurants offer a small choice of meals, while fifteen snack facilities provide a larger range of snack choices.

Season: Daily, April through mid-September; weekends through October; special Christmas hours, mid-December through mid-January.

Best day of the week to attend: Friday.

Hours: Open at 10 a.m. in summer and fall; open at 4 p.m. in winter.

Tickets: All day for one admission price: Adult, $7.95; children, $6.50; under 2, free; senior citizens discounts available.

Other Conveniences and Attractions: Arcade (150 games), petting zoo, parades, wildlife areas, picnic facilities, camping within 10 miles, camera rentals, wheelchairs and strollers, provisions made for handicapped, raincoats and sweatshirts for sale, lost and found, lost parents, first aid center, resting benches throughout the park, free maps of park, free parking with 1700 spaces available, break-down service, Master Charge and Visa accepted.

Other sites of interest are located within ten miles, including the Boston area and the Manchester area.

For further information write Benson's Animal Park, Rt. 111, Hudson NH 03051, or call (603) 882-2481.

Canobie Lake Park
Salem, New Hampshire

According to their brochure, Canobie Lake Park in Salem (southeastern New Hampshire) has been rated by an independent industry survey as one of the top ten most beautiful amusement centers in the nation. Situated on the shore of Canobie Lake, the park is just a short drive from Boston. The seventy-acre park is built on a flat terrain but does offer trees and covered waiting areas as protection from the sun.

Over thirty-eight rides are offered in the park, including three roller coasters, an antique carousel, a log flume and more. Nine shows are presented in various types of theaters, with top-name entertainment performing occasionally. Costumed characters and a high-dive show are part of the daily entertainment. Four shops offer souvenirs ranging in price from $1 to $30, with other goods at a higher price. One main restaurant and eight snack facilities offer a medium range of meal and snack choices. Service is good, as over ninety people are employed in concessions.

Season: Weekends, April and May; daily, June through Labor Day.

Hours: Opens at noon.

Tickets: All day for $9.00, or $2 admission plus charge for each ride.

Other Conveniences and Attractions: Arcade (150 games), parades, street shows, garden walks, locker rentals, wheelchairs and strollers, provisions made for handicapped, raincoats and sweatshirts for sale, lost and found, lost parents, first aid center, resting benches throughout the park, maps of park—at cost, covered waiting areas, free parking with 1700 spaces available, break-down service, fireworks (occasionally).

For further information write Canobie Lake Park, Salem NH 03079, or call (603) 893-3506.

Storyland
Glen, New Hampshire

Located in east central New Hampshire in the heart of the White Mountains, this small eighteen-acre park is a young-family attraction. Most of the attractions within the park are aimed at children ages two to twelve. The thirteen rides (three kiddie rides) are all based on a storybook theme, with costumed characters roaming the park. New attractions are added each year.

While considering the landscaping plans, the Morrell family decided to emphasize and maintain the natural scenery but add additional tree plantings, ponds and flower gardens. The area is, naturally, already heavily forested, with spectacular views of cliffs and peaks nearby.

Besides the views, landscaping and rides, the park offers four shops to provide souvenir hunters with prizes at a cost of $1 to $5. Two restaurants provide a medium range of meal choices, while the three snack concessions offer a small range of snack choices.

This picturesque park emphasizes friendly, courteous service and clean family entertainment.

Season: Daily, Father's Day to Labor Day; weekends, Labor Day to Columbus Day.

Hours: Opens at 9 a.m.

Best day to attend: Friday, Saturday, or Sunday.

Tickets: All day for $7.00.

Other Conveniences and Attractions: Arcade (2 games), 3 craftsmen at work, playground area, street shows, picnic facilities, camping within 10 miles, camera rentals, wheelchairs and strollers, provisions made for handicapped, raincoats and sweatshirts for sale, lost and found, lost parents, first aid center, resting benches throughout the park, maps of park — at cost, covered waiting areas, free parking with 600 spaces available.

Other sites of interest within forty miles include Santa's Village, Clark's Trading Post, Nature's Fantasy Farm and Lost River. Storyland belongs to the White Mountain Attraction Association, which consists of fifteen attractions, both natural and manmade, within a fifty-mile radius. This makes the area a popular resort area. For more information contact the White Mountains Attraction Association, Box 176, North Woodstock, NH 03262.

For further information write Storyland, Rt. 16, Box 1776, Glen NH 03838 or call (603) 383-4293.

Six Flags Great Adventure
Jackson, New Jersey

Located in central New Jersey, Six Flags Great Adventure entertainment complex claims to be the "nation's largest seasonal theme park, and the northeast's largest family entertainment center" (1983 brochure). The park sits on 1,700 acres of flat terrain. Landscaping was a major undertaking and is a constant concern of park management, with over thirty-seven people employed specifically in this area. Park cleanliness is also emphasized, with around 350 employed in this task.

The park offers more than forty-two rides (eleven kiddie rides), including the Sarajevo Bobsled, Roaring Rapids, FreeFall, Lightnin' Loops and more. Also included in the all-day admission is the drive-through Safari, with over 2,000 wild animals. Number of shows varies throughout the season, but there are usually from five to ten different shows each day. Top-name entertainment is always on the billing in at least one of the theaters. More than twenty-four shopping concessions provide plenty of shopping for items of all types and prices. Souvenirs range in price from 60¢ to $15. Three restaurants provide a medium range of meal choices, while around eighty-nine snack facilities provide a large range of snack choices.

Season: Daily, mid-April through mid-September; weekends through mid-October.

Hours: Opens at 10 a.m.

Best days to attend: Tuesday or Wednesday.

Tickets: All day for one admission price. Theme Park only, $14.79; Safari Park only, $5.25; combination of the two, $15.85.

Other Conveniences and Attractions: Arcade (394 games), 7 craftsmen at work, playground area, petting zoo, wildlife areas, picnic facilities, camping within 10 miles, pet care, camera rentals, locker rental, wheelchairs and strollers, provisions made for handicapped, raincoats and sweatshirts for sale, lost and found, lost parents, first aid center, resting benches throughout the park, posted maps of park, transportation from parking lot to park, 7800 parking spaces at a cost of $2, break-down service, fireworks (occasionally), most major credit cards accepted.

Other sites of interest nearby include historic sites in Philadelphia and New York City.

For further information write Six Flags Great Adventure, Rt. 537, Jackson NJ 08527. Call (201) 928-2000, or for a recording announcing special events, call (201) 928-3500.

Carowinds
Charlotte, North Carolina

Situated on the North Carolina/South Carolina border, Carowinds actually rests in the two states (two different sales tax rates are in effect). Visitors can walk the brick dividing line which meanders slightly through part of the park. The seventy-seven acre park rests on a flat terrain with beautiful landscaping, including many small flowerbeds and rock gardens ornamenting the walkways. Seven full-time employees, plus twelve seasonal employees, tend to the landscaping.

Carowinds is made up of eight different theme areas, each one depicting a different aspect of Carolina culture. Twenty-nine major rides (including seven roller coasters) and a few kiddie rides are located throughout the park, while a new "soft-play" area, Smurf Island, was added in 1984 especially for children. Carowinds originally opened in 1973 under the ownership of the Carowinds Corporation. The park was purchased in 1975 by Family Leisure Centers, Inc., a joint venture of Taft Broadcasting Company and the Kroger Company, both of Cincinnati, Ohio. Taft Broadcasting Company, which gained total control of the park in 1980, also operates Kings Island in Ohio and Kings Dominion in Virginia.

Twenty-seven shops provide a wide range of souvenir choices, with prices ranging from $1-up. Fifteen restaurants and thirty-two snack facilities offer a medium range of meal and snack choices. Unlike many large parks, these food concessions are located all over the park. Eight live shows are presented in various types of theaters, with facilities ranging from outside theaters with bench seats to air-conditioned theaters with individual seats.

Season: Weekends in March, April, May and September; daily except Friday, June through August.

Hours: Open at 10 a.m.

Best day to attend: Monday or Tuesday.

Tickets: All day for $11.95.

Other Conveniences and Attractions: Arcade (257 games), 6 crafts-men at work, picnic facilities, camping on premises, camping within 10 miles, pet care, camera rentals, locker rentals, wheelchairs and strollers, provisions made for handicapped, raincoats and sweatshirts for sale, lost and found, lost parents, first aid center, resting benches throughout the park, free maps of park, covered waiting areas, 43 acres of parking, at a cost of $2, break-down service, fireworks (July 4 only), major credit cards accepted.

Other sites of interest nearby include Andrew Jackson State Park, Charlotte Motor Speedway, Charlotte Nature Museum, Discovery Place Science Museum, James K. Polk Birthplace, Museum of Art, Museum of York County and Spirit Square.

For further information write Carowinds, P.O. Box 240516, Charlotte NC 28224, or call (704) 588-2606.

Ghost Town in the Sky
Maggie Valley, North Carolina

Ghost Town in the Sky is a seventy-acre park located in the extreme west of North Carolina, on top of a peak in the Smoky Mountains. Visitors can see spectacular views of the Smokies from most areas of the park. Entrance to the park is gained by a skyride to the top of the peak—nearly 900 feet up.

Although most famous for its shoot-outs and western theme, Ghost Town offers twenty amusement rides from which to choose. Thirteen shops offer souvenirs ranging in price from 50¢ to $20 and up. Five restaurants and six snack bars offer a medium range of meal and snack choices. Over thirty live shows are performed each day, rain or shine. Shows include an ice show, high-dive exhibition, shootouts, can-cans and more.

Season: May–October.

Hours: Opens at 9:30 a.m.

Best day to attend: Friday.

Tickets: All day for $8.95.

Other Conveniences and Attractions: Arcade (20 games), 6 craftsmen at work, street shows, garden walks, picnic facilities, camping within 10 miles, camera rentals, provisions made for handicapped, raincoats and sweatshirts for sale, lost and found, first aid center, rest benches throughout the park, free maps of park, transportation within the park, break-down service, fireworks, most major credit cards accepted.

Other sites of interest within thirty miles of the park include Gatlinburg, Tennessee, Great Smoky Mountains National Park and Santa's Land.

For further information write Ghost Town in the Sky, P.O. Box 790, Maggie Valley NC 28751, or call (704) 926-0256.

Santa's Land
Cherokee, North Carolina

This small twenty-five-acre park, located in the exteme west of North Carolina, is situated on the scenic Cherokee Indian Reservation, just three miles from the entrance to the Great Smoky Mountains National Park. Though Santa's Land does maintain the appeal of the mountainous countryside, walking is easy, as the park proper is built on flat terrain.

The park brochure boasts of "live entertainment, arts and crafts, rides and the largest zoo in the Smokies." Two shows are performed daily in bench-seated theaters; a variety of mountain crafts are exhibited; and eight rides are offered, mostly for the younger family members. Four shops within the park offer souvenirs ranging in price from 79¢ to $8. Mountain crafts are also for sale. Two restaurants offer a small range of meal choices, while two snack facilities offer a larger range of snack choices.

Season: May–October.

Best day to attend: Thursday or Friday.

Tickets: All day for one admission price: Adults, $6.95; children, $5.95.

Other Conveniences and Attractions: Arcade (6 games), 5 craftsmen at work, playground area, petting zoo, garden walks, wildlife areas, picnic facilities, camping within 10 miles, provisions made for handicapped, raincoats and sweatshirts for sale, lost and found, lost parents, resting benches throughout the park, free maps of park, covered waiting areas, free parking with 300 spaces available, Master-Card and Visa accepted.

Other sites of interest nearby include Gatlinburg, Knoxville, and the Smoky Mountains National Park (all in Tennessee), and the Cherokee Indian Reservation.

For further information write Santa's Land, Cherokee NC 28719, or call (704) 497-9191.

Cedar Point
Sandusky, Ohio

Cedar Point is an older, traditional amusement park located in northwestern Ohio on the shore of Lake Erie. The 365-acre park offers some beautiful scenic sites, as it is surrounded by water on three sides. Flat terrain makes walking easy.

Besides the fifty-four major rides and sixteen kiddie rides (including six coasters and five carousels), the park also includes a marina, public bathing beach and the historic Hotel Breakers (opened in 1905). The park is a blend of old-fashioned grandeur and new-fashioned fun, with live animal shows, a new river rafting ride, and a futuristic IMAX movie offering new thrills for all ages.

Picnicking and family fun have been among the park's major attractions since the park opened in 1870. Fourteen restaurants provide a variety of meal choices. Five live shows are performed daily, although top-name entertainment is never on the billing. Many shops provide ample choices for souvenir hunters.

Cedar Point is a sister park to Valleyfair in Shakopee, Minnesota, both being operated by Cedar Fair Limited Partnership.

Season: Every day, May 10 through Labor Day, and the following two weekends.

Best days to attend: Weekdays.

Tickets: All day for one admission price: Adults (9–59), $14.95; ages 4–8, $8.95; senior citizens (60 and over), $9.95; 3 and under are free. Two-day passes are $23.75; special admission after 5 p.m., $8.50.

Other Conveniences and Attractions: Arcade (400 games), 12 craftsmen at work, playground area, petting zoo, street shows, wildlife areas, picnic facilities, camping on premises (RV only), camping within 10 miles, pet care, camera rentals, locker rentals, wheelchairs and strollers, provisions made for handicapped, raincoats and sweatshirts for sale within the park, lost and found, lost parents, first aid center, resting benches throughout the park, maps of park (free and at cost), 16 restrooms, transportation from parking lot to park, 15,000 parking spaces at a cost of $2, breakdown service available, fireworks (special occasions only), most major credit cards accepted.

Other sites of interest include the many Lake Erie attractions.

For further information write Cedar Point, C.N. 5006, Sandusky OH 44870, or call (419) 626-0830.

Geauga Lake
Aurora, Ohio

Located in northwestern Ohio, Geauga Lake is a formal amusement park. Originally a trolley park, the management has spent over $5,000,000 to renovate and expand the facilities, until the present modern park is one of the largest in a several-state area. Covering 175 beautifully wooded, slightly hilly acres, the park employs sixteen people specifically to maintain the landscaping, both natural and man-made. The park offers both trees and covered waiting areas as protection from the hot summer sun.

Over fifty-two rides (seventeen kiddie rides) are available, along with miniature golf, a western village building, a ballroom and a "Boardwalk Shores" area, which is a small water-fun park. Four shops within the park offer souvenirs ranging in price from 50¢ to $500. Three restaurants offer a medium range of meal choices, while twenty-two snack stands offer a small range of snack choices. Five live shows are presented daily in theaters of all types, although top-name entertainment is never on the billing.

Season: Daily from the end of May through Labor Day; weekends, May and September.

Hours: Opens at 10 a.m.

Tickets: All day for $9.95.

Other Conveniences and Attractions: Arcade (250 games), 3 craftsmen at work, picnic facilities, camping within 10 miles, camera rentals, locker rentals, wheelchairs and strollers, provisions made for handicapped, raincoats and sweatshirts for sale, lost and found, lost parents, first aid center, resting benches throughout the park, free maps of park, covered waiting areas, 4000 parking spaces at a cost of $1, break-down service, most major credit cards accepted.

Other sites of interest within seventy miles include Cedar Point Park, Sea World of Ohio and Idora Park.

For further information write Geauga Lake, 1060 Aurora Rd., Aurora OH 44202, or call (216) 562-7131.

Idora Park
Youngstown, Ohio

Idora Park is located in Youngstown's Mill Creek Park in mideastern Ohio. The fifty-acre park includes picnic areas, rides and concessions. Although the park is only midsized, offering twenty major rides and fourteen kiddie rides, it can boast of two famous attractions: The Wildcat Roller Coaster, which has been rated among the top ten in the country by Gary Kyriazi, author of the book *The Great American Amusement Parks*; and the Merry-go-round, built in 1922, which was placed on the National Register of Historical Places in 1975 by the National Park Service.

One main restaurant and nine refreshment stands offer a medium range of meal and snack choices. The Idora Ballroom occasionally offers top-name entertainment on Wednesday and Saturday nights.

Season: Weekends, May through mid-June; Thurs–Sun, mid-June through Labor Day.

Hours: Opens at 1 p.m.

Tickets: All day for $6.95, or $2 general admission and $3 for 10 universal ride tickets.

Other Conveniences and Attractions: Street shows, picnic facilities, camping within 10 miles, provisions made for handicapped, raincoats and sweatshirts for sale, lost and found, lost parents, first aid center, resting benches throughout the park, free parking, break-down service.

For further information write Idora Park, P.O. Box 3008, Youngstown OH 44511, or call (216) 782-1162.

Kings Island
Kings Island, Ohio

Located in southwestern Ohio, just north of Cincinnati, Kings Island is one of the major theme parks in the nation. Beautifully landscaped and maintained, the park features several themes: International Street, Oktoberfest, Coney Island, African Safari, Rivertown and The Happy Land of Hanna-Barbera. The many roller coasters and other rides offer a fast-paced, full day of riding thrills.

Ten live shows are presented daily in theaters of all types, ranging from bench-seat theaters to air-conditioned theaters with individual padded seats. Top-name entertainers perform occasionally, along with the first-rate regular performers. Eleven restaurants and numerous snack concessions offer a huge range of shopping pleasures, with smaller souvenirs ranging in price from 50¢ up.

Kings Island is one of the three parks presently owned and operated by the Family Leisure Centers, Inc., a division of Taft

eautiful picnic groves and a giant olympic-sized pool are at-
ffered in addition to the midway.

idway offers eighteen major rides (eight kiddie rides), plus
golf, an arcade and games of skill. One restaurant and one
ity offer some range of meal and snack choices. One shop
all range of souvenir choices. Fireworks are provided on
no live shows are regularly scheduled.

ot available).

to attend: Tuesday and Thursday.

ens at 1:00 p.m.

o admission charge; each ride 50¢. Half-price on Tuesday
day.

nveniences and Attractions: Arcade (65 games), picnic
camping within 10 miles, provisions made for the handi-
st and found, lost parents, first aid center, resting benches
t the park, free parking with 500 spaces available, break-
ice.

ite within fifty miles is Dorney Park.

r information write Angela Park, P.O. Box 611, Hazelton
, or call (717) 788-2325 or (717) 455-1511.

Bland Park
Tipton, Pennsylvania

d Park is a very small (eight-acre) family park located in
n Pennsylvania. Advertising "old-fashioned fun at family
he park contains twelve major rides and two kiddie rides,
ntique Herschell–Spillman carousel and miniature steam-
locomotive being two main attractions. One shop offers
ranging in price from $1 to $5. Two restaurants and several
cessions offer a medium range of meal and snack choices.
ght shows are offered each season, with top-name entertain-
g occasionally on the billing.

Broadcasting Company. (Carowinds in North Carolina and Kings Dominion in Virginia are the other two.)

Season: Daily, Memorial Day to Labor Day; selected weekends in April, May, Sept and Oct.

Hours: Opens at 9 a.m.

Tickets: All day for one admission price: Adults, $13.50; ages 3–6, $6.75; under 3, free.

Other Conveniences and Attractions: Playground area, petting zoo, parades, street shows, garden walks, wildlife areas, picnic facilities, camping on premises, camping within 10 miles, camera rentals, locker rentals, wheelchairs and strollers, provisions made for handicapped, raincoats and sweatshirts for sale, lost and found, lost parents, first aid center, resting benches throughout the park, transportation from parking lot to park, covered waiting areas, plenty of parking spaces at a cost of $2, fireworks (occasionally), most major credit cards accepted.

Other sites of interest nearby include the College Football Hall of Fame (next door), the Cincinnati Zoo and other Cincinnati attractions.

For further information write Kings Island, P.O. Box 400, Kings Island OH 45034, or call toll-free 1-800-582-3051 (inside Ohio) or 1-800-543-4031 (outside Ohio).

Sea World
Aurora, Ohio

Located in northeastern Ohio near Cleveland, Sea World is an eighty-five-acre marine life park and entertainment center, the only one of its kind in mid-America. Sitting on a sloping terrain, the park is beautifully landscaped and maintained, with up to seventy people employed specifically for those tasks. Both trees and covered waiting areas help provide shelter from the elements. (For more information, see Sea World in Orlando, Florida.)

Sea World offers more than twenty attractions, shows and exhibits, including a two and one-half-acre children's play area built around a nautical theme. Over seven live shows are performed several times daily, with fireworks and top-name entertainment occasionally on the billing. All theaters contain bench- or bleacher-type seats, but are covered to enable park visitors to view the shows regardless of the weather.

Twenty shops offer a range of shopping pleasures, with souvenirs ranging in price from 50¢ to $1,000. Two restaurants offer a medium–large range of meal choices, while thirty snack facilities offer a large range of snack choices. Over 155 people are employed in the restaurants and over 300 work in snack concessions.

Season: Late May through early September.

Hours: Opens at 9 a.m.

Best day to attend: Friday.

Tickets: All day for one admission price: Ages 12 and older, $10.95; ages 3–11, $9.95; ages 60 and older, $8.50; under 3, free.

Other Conveniences and Attractions: Arcade (50 games), playground area, petting zoo, wildlife areas, picnic facilities, camping within 10 miles, guide service available, camera rentals, locker rentals, wheelchairs and strollers, provisions made for handicapped, raincoats and sweatshirts for sale, lost and found, lost parents, first aid center, resting benches throughout the park, free maps of park, covered waiting areas, free parking with 7100 spaces available, break-down service, fireworks (occasionally), most major credit cards accepted.

Other sites of interest nearby include Geauga Lake Amusement Park and the Cleveland Area.

For further information write Sea World, 1100 Sea World Dr., Aurora OH 44202, or call (216) 562-8101.

White Water
Oklahoma City, Oklahoma

A family outdoor water-fun park.

For further information, see White W... write White Water Park, Oklahoma C...

Enchanted
Turner, Or...

Opened in 1971, seven miles south ... park is built around a storybook theme. ... a natural setting of beautiful trees, shr...

The park's creator, Roger Tofte, p... development. Presently catering mostly ... offer one Coney Island–type ride and oth... is performed five times daily outdoors. ... feature souvenirs ranging in price from ... three snack concessions offer a small ch...

Season: March 15–September 30.

Best day to attend: Tuesday or Wednes...

Hours: Opens at 9:30 a.m.

Tickets: All day for one admission price: ... $3.00.

Other Conveniences and Attractions: Pic... 10 miles, raincoats and sweatshirts for s... found, first aid center, resting benches thr... of park, transportation within the park, ...

For further information write Enchant... Way SE, Turner OR 97392.

Angela P...
Hazelton, Penns...

Located six miles north of Hazelton, ... claims to be "northeast Pennsylvania's s...

parking, ... tractions ...

The ... miniature ... snack fac... offers a s... July 4, b...

Season: (...

Best day: ...

Hours: C...

Tickets: ... and Thu...

Other C... facilities, ... capped, ... througho... down se...

Another ...

For furt... PA 1820...

Bla... midwest ... prices," ... with an ... powered... souvenir... snack co... Five to e... ment be...

Season: Sundays in May and September; Wed–Sun in June, July and August.

Best day to attend: Wednesday or Saturday.

Hours: Opens at 1:00 p.m. Wednesday, Saturday and Sunday; 5:00 p.m. Thursday and Friday.

Tickets: No admission; 20¢ per ticket. Pay one price ($1.95) Fridays 5:00 p.m.–9:00 p.m.

Other Conveniences and Attractions: Arcade (30 games), picnic facilities, camping within 10 miles, lost and found, lost parents, first aid center, resting benches throughout the park, free maps of park, free parking with 500 spaces available, fireworks, miniature golf.

Other sites of interest located within twenty miles include all the Pittsburgh area amusements.

For further information write Bland Park, Rt. 220, Tipton PA 16684, or call (814) 684-3538.

Conneaut Lake Park
Conneaut Lake Park, Pennsylvania

Located in northwestern Pennsylvania on the shore of the state's largest spring-fed lake, Conneaut Lake Park is more than just an amusement park. A turn-of-the-century hotel, nearby golf course and beaches offering a variety of water activities are readily available for the pleasure of park visitors.

The amusement park area offers more than forty rides (twelve kiddie rides), along with a shooting gallery, skill games and an arcade. Dozens of food concessions offer a medium–large variety of meal and snack choices. Live entertainment is available at both the park and the hotel. A new children's play area was added in 1984.

Season: All summer.

Tickets: No admission price, but a charge for each ride.

Other Conveniences and Attractions: Arcade, playground area, petting zoo, street shows, picnic facilities, resting benches throughout the park, free parking, MasterCard and Visa accepted.

Other sites of interest include the Erie area, located nearby.

For further information write Conneaut Lake Park, Inc., Conneaut Lake PA 16316, or call (814) 382-5115.

Dorney Park
Allentown, Pennsylvania

Located in the heart of Pennsylvania Dutch Country in mideastern Pennsylvania, Dorney Park celebrated its one-hundredth anniversary in 1984. A nineteenth-century mansion, once owned by Solomon Dorney, has been converted into an old-time food and craft center. Situated on 163 rolling acres, the park has trees and covered waiting areas to help protect visitors from the sun. Fifteen major rides and seven kiddie rides provide both old- and new-fashioned thrills. Ten shops within the park offer plenty of shopping. Two restaurants and twenty-one snack concessions offer a large range of meal and snack choices. Five live shows are presented each day in the air-conditioned theater, with top-name entertainment performing occasionally.

Season: Weekends, April to mid-May; daily except Monday and Tuesday in June; daily in July and August.

Best days to attend: Weekdays.

Hours: Opens at noon.

Tickets: $2.00 admission tickets plus 20¢ each ticket (rides require 2–6 tickets), or all day for one price: Adults, $9.00; ages 4 and under, $4.00.

Other Conveniences and Attractions: Arcade (50 games), 10 craftsmen at work, street shows, picnic facilities, camping within 10 miles, wheelchairs and strollers, provisions made for handicapped, lost and found, lost parents, first aid center, resting benches throughout the park, free maps of park, covered waiting areas, 3000 parking spaces at a cost of 50¢, break-down service, most major credit cards accepted.

Another site of interest is Angela Park, located within eighty miles.

For further information write Dorney Park, Allentown PA 18101, or call (215) 395-3724.

Dutch Wonderland
Lancaster, Pennsylvania

Dutch Wonderland is a small (forty-four-acre) family park located in southeastern Pennsylvania. Situated beside a large stream, the park sits on a gently sloped terrain, with many trees providing ample shade. The park is beautifully landscaped and tended, with over thirty-six people employed specifically for those tasks. Free parking is readily available, with over 1200 parking spaces provided.

The park opened in 1963 with four rides sitting on fourteen acres. A boat tour on the stream was (and is) one of the most popular rides. Picnicking and relaxing were once the main attractions. Since that time, the park has added at least one major attraction each year, the most recent being several acres of flower gardens. This theme area also contains three kiddie rides. Another special feature in the park is its handcarved miniature circus display.

Two live shows are performed several times daily, the themes of which change each year. In 1984 the shows were a high-dive exhibition outside and a circus performed inside an air-conditioned building. Three restaurants and four snack stands provide a small variety of meals; picnicking under the trees is still encouraged. Five shops located throughout the park offer a large range of souvenir choices, ranging in price from 25¢ to $250.

Season: Weekends in the spring and fall; daily from Memorial Day to Labor Day.

Best day to attend: Friday.

Tickets: $5.80 for admission and a few rides (extra tickets can be purchased for other rides); or $8.80 for an all-day admission.

Other Conveniences and Attractions: Arcade (22 games), craftsman, playground areas, petting zoo, garden walks, maps of park at cost, picnic facilities, wheelchairs and stroller, raincoats and sweatshirts for sale, lost and found, lost parents, first aid center, resting benches throughout the park, transportation from parking lot to park, most major credit cards accepted.

Other sites of interest within fifty miles of the park are many. Some sites include the National Wax Museum (adjacent to the park) and the Pennsylvania Dutch Historic sites of interest. Camping facilities are also located adjacent to the park.

For further information write Dutch Wonderland, 2249 Lincoln Hwy. E, Lancaster PA 17602, or call (717) 291-1888.

Hersheypark
Hershey, Pennsylvania

Located in southeastern Pennsylvania, Hersheypark sits on eighty-one acres of beautiful, green, rolling countryside. Scenery is a major concern of the management, with each ride appropriately landscaped and tended.

The park offers thirty-nine rides (thirteen kiddie rides), including an antique carousel, the Comet (one of the top-rated roller coasters in the nation), the SooperDooperLooper coaster and the Trailblazer coaster. Fifteen shops within the park offer plenty of shopping, with souvenirs ranging in price from 25¢ to $300. Six restaurants and over fifty snack concessions offer a wide range of meal and snack choices, with snack concessions located all over the park. Six live shows are presented daily, with top-name entertainment always on the billing somewhere.

Season: Weekends in May and September; daily from the last week in May through Labor Day.

Best days to attend: Tuesday–Thursday.

Hours: Opens at 10:30 a.m.

Tickets: All day for one admission price: Adults (ages 9–61), $13.95; juniors (ages 5–8), $10.95; senior citizens (ages 62 and over), $7.95; 4 and under, free.

Other Conveniences and Attractions: 7 craftsmen at work, playground area, parades, garden walks (23 acres), wildlife areas, picnic facilities, camping within 10 miles, pet care, locker rentals, wheelchairs and strollers, provisions made for handicapped, raincoats and sweatshirts for sale within the park, lost and found, lost parents, first aid center, resting benches throughout the park, free maps of park, transportation from the parking lot to the park, covered waiting areas, free parking with 8000 spaces available, break-down service, fireworks (July 4), Hershey Museum of American Life, two hotels, most major credit cards accepted.

Other sites of interest within ninety miles include Chocolate World (Hershey's visitor center) and Founders Hall (next door and free of charge), Dutch Wonderland and the Harrisburg area.

For further information write Hersheypark, 100 W. Hersheypark Dr., Hershey PA 17033, or call (717) 534-3916.

Kennywood
West Mifflin, Pennsylvania

Located ten miles from downtown Pittsburgh, Kennywood is a beautifully landscaped traditional amusement park, which boasts of being the "roller coaster capital of the world." Situated on 115 acres (forty park proper, seventy-five acres free parking), the park features thirty-one major rides and twelve kiddie rides, with four of the major rides and one kiddie ride being roller coasters. Although there are parks around the country which do have more coasters, roller coaster enthusiasts will not be disappointed at Kennywood. One of the coasters, the Thunderbolt, has been rated #1 in the world by one roller coaster enthusiasts' group.

One major restaurant offers a medium range of meal choices,

while fifteen snack stands offer a wide range of snack choices. Snack stands are located evenly throughout the park. Live entertainment is offered daily, although top-name entertainment is never on the billing.

Season: May 11 through Labor Day; closed Mondays between July 4 and Labor Day.

Hours: Opens at noon.

Tickets: $1.50 admission plus 20¢ tickets (rides require 2 or 3 tickets); or on specified dates, all day for $9.95.

Other Conveniences and Attractions: Arcade (38 games), parades, garden walks, picnic facilities, locker rentals, wheelchairs and strollers, provisions made for handicapped, raincoats and sweatshirts for sale within the park, lost and found, first aid center, resting benches throughout the park, covered waiting areas, free parking, parking spaces available at a cost of $1.50.

Other sites of interest are located within thirty miles throughout the Pittsburgh area.

For further information write Kennywood Park, 4800 Kennywood Blvd., West Mifflin PA 15122, or call (412) 461-0500.

Knoebels Amusement Resort
Elysburg, Pennsylvania

Located in east central Pennsylvania, Knoebels Amusement Resort rests on sixty acres of hardwood, pine and hemlock forest. The natural beauty of these woods has been maintained as much as possible, as camping is a major attraction of the resort facility. Other resort attractions include "Pennsylvania's largest swimming pool complex" (with a ¾-million gallon pool), tennis courts, basketball courts, hiking, two giant water slides and over two acres of sunning area.

The amusement park proper offers thirty major rides and one visual ride (included are twelve kiddie rides). Seven shops within the park offer a variety of shopping, with souvenirs ranging in price from

$1 to $8. Two restaurants and nine snack concessions offer a medium–large range of meal and snack choices. Two live shows are presented daily, although top-name entertainment is never on the billing.

Season: Daily, Memorial Day to Labor Day; certain weekends in May and September.

Hours: Opens at 11:00 a.m.

Tickets: No admission; rides cost 20¢ to $1.00.

Other Conveniences and Attractions: Arcade (50 games), 6 craftsmen at work, playground area, petting zoo, street shows, picnic facilities, camping on premises, camera rentals, locker rentals, wheelchairs and strollers, provisions made for handicapped, raincoats and sweatshirts for sale, lost and found, lost parents, first aid center, resting benches throughout the park, free maps of park, transportation from parking lot to park, covered waiting areas, free parking with 4000 spaces available, break-down service.

For further information write Knoebels Amusement Resort, Elysburg PA 17824, or call (717) 672-2572.

Trout Pond Park
Muncy, Pennsylvania

This very small family park is located in east central Pennsylvania on twenty-five acres of flat terrain. Trees and covered waiting areas help provide shelter from the hot summer sun. Because of its size, Trout Pond has few traveling tourists and so caters mostly to local clientele. Woods surround most of the facility, where picnicking is a major attraction. Besides four rides, the park offers a gift shop, an outdoor theater, arcade, skating rink, dance hall, snack stands and playground area.

Season: Memorial Day until the Sunday after Labor Day.

Best day to attend: Sunday.

Tickets: No admission; rides $1 to $1.40.

Other Conveniences and Attractions: Arcade (10 games), playground area, picnic facilities, camping on premises, guide service available, provisions made for handicapped, raincoats and sweatshirts for sale, lost and found, lost parents, first aid center, resting benches throughout the park, covered waiting areas, free parking available.

Other sites of interest nearby are Kennywood Park and the Pittsburgh area.

For further information write Trout Pond Park, RFD #5, Box 466, Muncy PA 17756.

Willow Mill Park
Mechanicsburg, Pennsylvania

Located in south central Pennsylvania, this twenty-one-acre park sits on a slightly hilly terrain, where the natural tree cover helps provide shade while waiting in line for the rides. Nineteen major rides and one live animal ride are available. Ten live shows are performed daily in outdoor theaters, although top-name entertainment is never on the billing.

One shop in the park offers souvenirs ranging in price from 50¢ to $5.00. Six food stands offer a small range of meal choices, but a medium–large range of snack choices.

Season: Daily except Friday, Father's Day to Labor Day; weekends, May, early June and September.

Hours: Opens at 12:30 p.m.

Tickets: All day for one admission price: $5.75 weekends; $4.75 weekdays; or pay no admission, purchase 10¢ tickets (rides require multiple tickets).

Other Conveniences and Attractions: Arcade (100 games), 1 craftsman at work, picnic facilities, camping within 10 miles, wheelchairs and strollers, provisions made for handicapped, lost and found, lost parents, first aid center, resting benches throughout the park, free parking, break-down service.

Other sites of interest within fifty miles, including other amusement parks and the Harrisburg area.

For further information write Willow Mill Park, Willow Mill Park Rd., Mechanicsburg PA 17055, or call (717) 766-9639.

Magic Harbor
Myrtle Beach, South Carolina

Located in the huge resort area of Myrtle Beach, Magic Harbor is the largest amusement park on the south Atlantic coast. Magic Mountain, next door, is a part of the forty-four-acre complex, but operates under separate admission prices and at different times.

The amusement park proper offers twenty-three major rides, one of which is the largest ferris wheel in the nation. A live elephant ride is an additional attraction. Seven shops offer plenty of shopping, with souvenirs ranging in price from 50¢ to $30. While there are no restaurants in the park, several specialty food shops offer a medium range of snack choices. Beautiful picnic facilities are located along the beach area. Four live shows are presented a few times each day, top-name entertainment occasionally on the billing (theaters are not air-conditioned).

Season: Weekends, spring and fall; daily, May 27–September 5.

Best days to attend: Monday through Wednesday.

Hours: 4:00 p.m. to midnight.

Tickets: All day for one admission price: Adults, $6.75; ages 5–12, $5.75; 4 and under, free.

Other Conveniences and Attractions: Arcade (30 games), playground area, garden walks, wildlife areas, picnic facilities, camping within 10 miles, locker rentals, wheelchairs and strollers, provisions made for handicapped, raincoats and sweatshirts for sale, lost and found, lost parents, first aid center, resting benches throughout the park, break-down service, fireworks, MasterCard and Visa accepted.

Other amusements within ten miles include Magic Mountain Water Park, Grand Strand Amusement Park, Surfside Amusement Park, Sun Fun Amusement Park and nearby Atlantic beaches.

For further information contact Magic Harbor, 4901 South Kings Highway, Myrtle Beach SC 29577, or call (803) 238-0717.

Carowinds
South Carolina

(See Carowinds, North Carolina.)

Libertyland Theme Park
Memphis, Tennessee

Located in the southwestern corner of Tennessee (right in the heart of Memphis) this twenty-three-acre theme park is a mixture of amusement, education and history (the park's official grand opening was July 4, 1976). Landscaping is a major concern of the park, which employs three professional horticulturists and a full-time grounds crew during the operating season. Over 800 hanging baskets both receive and draw special attention, along with two large waterfalls. The park has a goal to make Libertyland the "Garden Spot of the City."

The park is divided into three main theme areas: Colonial Land, Turn-of-the-Century Land and Frontier Land. Each area has its own rides, landscaping and atmosphere. Cleanliness is evident throughout the park. Eleven major rides and three kiddie rides (including visual, amusement-type, water rides and live animal rides) provide a full day of riding thrills. Shoppers can spend lots of time in the park's ten shops, where souvenirs range in price from $1 to $12. Two restaurants and twenty-four snack facilities provide a medium range of meal and snack choices. Snack facilities are evenly spaced throughout the park. Seven shows are performed daily, including a dolphin show. Theaters include both bench-type seats outdoors and cane-back chairs indoors. Well-known local talent is occasionally on the billing, along with periodic special events.

Season: Weekends in April, May, late August and early September; daily, June through mid-August.

Best days to attend: Thursday and Friday.

Hours: Opens at 11:00 a.m.—Sunday at noon.

Tickets: All day for one admission price: Adults, $8.75; senior citizens, $5.00; 3 and under, free.

Other Conveniences and Attractions: Arcade (15 games), 2 craftsmen at work, playground area, petting zoo, street shows, picnic facilities, camping within 10 miles, camera rentals, wheelchairs and strollers, provisions made for handicapped, raincoats and sweatshirts for sale, lost and found, lost parents, first aid center, resting benches throughout the park, maps of park at cost, break-down service, most major credit cards accepted.

There are many sites of interest in the Memphis area.

For further information write Libertyland Theme Park, Mid-South Fairgrounds, 940 Early Maxwell Blvd., Memphis TN 37104, or call (901) 274-1776.

Opryland, U.S.A.
Nashville, Tennessee

Located just outside of Nashville on 120 acres of flat terrain, Opryland obviously takes its name from the theater that has drawn so many people to its doors—The Grand Ole Opry. And, indeed, the New Grand Ole Opryhouse, located just outside the park entrance, continues to draw the crowds. Although admission to the Grand Ole Opry program itself requires a separate ticket, there are some live shows performed there daily to which park visitors are allowed free admission. Some Nashville Network shows taped there also allow park visitors free admission with the price of their tickets. These shows include *Nashville Now* and *Hee Haw*.

Opened in the early 1970s, with a definite musical theme, the park now offers a total of twenty-eight major rides (thirteen adult, fifteen kiddie), and more than twelve live shows performed daily throughout the park (more than most other parks). These shows are offered in a variety of settings, from air-conditioned theaters to open-air, tree-shaded, bench-seated amphitheaters. Top-name entertainment is continually on the billing. Twenty restaurants and numerous snack facilities offer an adequate range of meal choices, while many shops offer a large choice of souvenirs (mostly country and western).

Season: Late May to early September: Daily; weekends only, late March to late May, and early September to early November.

Best days to attend: Weekdays.

Tickets: All day for one admission price: $16.11 (tax included). Parkgoers may receive a second day free if they ask for a two-day ticket (be sure to ask if it is free before purchasing the ticket).

Other Conveniences and Attractions: Arcade (100 games), craftsmen at work, playground area, petting zoo, wildlife areas, picnic facilities, 5 campgrounds within ½ mile, pet care ($1 a day), camera rentals, locker rentals, wheelchairs and strollers, provisions made for handicapped, raincoats and sweatshirts for sale within the park, lost and found, lost parents, first aid center, resting benches throughout the park, free maps of park, 5 restrooms, transportation from parking lot to park, transportation within the park, covered waiting areas, parking available at a cost of $2, breakdown service available, fireworks on July 4, costumed characters, separate admissions for a new boat ride (includes dinner & show cruise).

Other sites of interest include the many tourist attractions in the Nashville area, such as stars' homes, Country-Music Stars Hall of Fame, and many more.

For further information write Opryland, U.S.A., 2802 Opryland Drive, Nashville TN 37214 or call (615) 889-6600.

Pigeon Forge
Pigeon Forge, Tennessee

Although not strictly classifiable as an amusement park, Pigeon Forge, in east central Tennessee, nevertheless provides days of amusement pleasures. We think that this is one of the most unique atmospheres in amusement history—an entire town dedicated to providing an attraction-packed family vacation. Over thirty-six attractions are available in the form of small parks within the "park-town." Attractions include golf and miniature golf, petting zoos, four-wheeler rides, bumper cars, several water-slide miniparks (one with an elevator), museums, ski shows, helicopter rides, roller skating, wave pools, craftsmen at work, animal shows, several thrill rides and more.

Shopping is plentiful within each minipark and as separate facilities. There are over forty-two motels (with 3600 rooms), 1600 campsites, and several family-style restaurants, which mostly advertise down-home cooking.

Season: Varies with attraction.

Hours: Varies with attraction.

Tickets: No admission charge; charge for each attraction.

Other Conveniences and Attractions: Craftsmen at work, playground area, petting zoo, parades, garden walks, wildlife areas, picnic facilities, camping within 10 miles, guide service available, maps of park—free and at cost, transportation from parking lot to park, transportation within the park, break-down service.

Other sites of interest nearby are the Great Smoky Mountains and the Gatlinburg, Tennessee, area.

For further information write Pigeon Forge, P.O. Box 209-E, Pigeon Forge TN 37863.

AstroWorld
Houston, Texas

AstroWorld, located in Houston, Texas, is a seventy-five-acre family theme park which offers over 100 rides, shows and attractions in its twelve different theme areas. Originally opened in 1968 by a private individual, AstroWorld was taken over in 1975 by Six Flags Corporation, now a Bally Company.

Landscaping in the park is a major undertaking, with over twenty-four people employed specifically for this task. Over 600 varieties of shrubs, flowers, plants and hanging baskets adorn the park and provide shaded areas for relief from the sun. These plants were purposefully picked to complement the theme of each section of the park.

Thirty rides (nine kiddie rides) offer thrills to ride enthusiasts of all ages. Fourteen shows are offered daily in air-conditioned theaters and outdoors, with top-name entertainers always on the billing. AstroWorld claims three unique features: the Number One roller coaster in the world (Texas Cyclone), an entire section devoted to parent/child interaction (Enchanted Kingdom), and an original 1895 Dentzel Carousel. Twenty-five shops offer ample shopping opportunities, with souvenirs ranging in price from $1.50 to $20. Four restaurants (employing eighty people) and forty snack facilities (employing 470 people) offer a large range of food choices.

Season: Weekends, March through May and September through November; daily, end of May to September.

Best day to attend: Tuesday.

Tickets: All day for $13.50.

Other Conveniences and Attractions: Arcade (210 games), 20 craftsmen at work, parades, street shows, garden walks, wildlife areas, picnic facilities, guide service available, camera rentals, locker rentals, wheelchairs and strollers, provisions made for handicapped, raincoats and sweatshirts for sale, lost and found, lost parents, first aid center, resting benches throughout the park, maps of park at cost, transportation from parking lot to park, transportation within the park, covered

waiting areas, 5000 parking spaces at a cost of $3, fireworks (occasionally), check cashing service, most major credit cards accepted.

Other sites of interest within twenty miles of the park include Fine Arts Museum, Museum of Natural Science, Hanna-Barbera Land, the Astrodome and NASA.

For further information write AstroWorld, 9001 Kirby Drive, Houston TX 77054, or call (713) 748-1234 or 1-800-241-0683.

International Wildlife Park
Grand Prairie, Texas

This world-famous park is both a wildlife preserve, featuring more than 2,500 exotic animals, and an entertainment village featuring rides on elephants, camels, bumper boats, paddle boats and a train. Petting zoos, special exhibits and animal shows are also provided in the beautifully manicured park. 1985 brought two new additions: a minicircus and a reptile exhibit on the riverboat ride.

Nine shows are performed daily, some in air-conditioned theaters and some in outdoor stadiums. Top-name entertainment is occasionally on the billing. One large shop provides souvenirs of all kinds, in all price ranges. Two restaurants and two snack facilities offer a medium range of meal and snack choices.

Season: March through November.

Tickets: All day for $8.95.

Other Conveniences and Attractions: Arcade games, playground area, petting zoo, wildlife areas, picnic facilities, camping within 10 miles, pet care, camera rentals, wheelchairs and strollers, provisions for handicapped, raincoats and sweatshirts for sale, lost and found, first aid center, resting benches throughout the park, free maps of park, covered waiting areas, free parking, break-down service, most major credit cards accepted.

Other sites of interest within ten miles of the park include White

Water, Wet'n'Wild, Six Flags, Sports Hall of Fame and a wax museum.

For further information write International Wildlife Park, 601 Wildlife Parkway, Grand Prairie TX 75050, or call (214) 263-2201.

Six Flags over Texas
Arlington, Texas

Six Flags over Texas is another of the Six Flags chain of major amusement parks. Situated on 205 slightly hilly acres, the wooded terrain offers shade while walking, and many of the rides have covered waiting areas for the parkgoers' protection while waiting in line.

Thirty major rides and seven kiddie rides provide a full day of riding excitement, while more than thirty-six restaurants and concession stands offer plenty of eating pleasures. Seven live shows are presented throughout the park each day. Top-name entertainment is often on the billing (at an extra charge). We suggest that you check with the park ahead of time to reserve seats for these performances.

This park was the first regional theme park in the area, opening in 1961.

Season: March through October (weekends in the spring and fall; daily all summer).

Best days to attend: Tuesday, Wednesday and Thursday.

Tickets: All day for one admission price: adults, $14.95; children under 42", $7.95; senior citizens (55 and older), $9.95.

Other Conveniences and Attractions: Arcade (50 games), 3 craftsmen at work, playground area, parades (summer evenings), street shows, picnic facilities, camping within 10 miles, pet care, camera rentals, locker rentals, wheelchairs and strollers, provisions made for handicapped, raincoats and sweatshirts for sale within the park, lost and found, lost parents, first aid center, resting benches throughout the park, maps of park (at cost), transportation from parking lot to park, 6500 parking spaces at a cost of $3, break-down service available, fireworks on occasion, most major credit cards accepted.

Other sites of interest close by include the Dallas/Ft. Worth area sites.

For further information write Six Flags over Texas, Arlington TX 76010, or call (817) 640-8900.

White Water
Garland, Texas

A family outdoor water-fun park.

For further information, see White Water Park, Grand Prairie, Texas, or write White Water Park, Garland TX 75050.

White Water
Grand Prairie, Texas

White Water Park, located about six miles from Six Flags in Grand Prairie, is one of five family water parks operating under the White Water Company. Opened in 1982, the Grand Prairie park was the third, but not the last park to be opened. Other parks are located in Garland, Texas; Atlanta, Georgia; Oklahoma City, Oklahoma; and Branson, Missouri.

White Water parks offer water slides, water rapids, a wave pool, children's play area, lounging areas, refreshment stands, gift shops, high-dive team exhibition, and nightly entertainment. (Each park differs slightly. Be sure to correspond with the individual park for further information before visiting.)

Season: Daily, Memorial Day to Labor Day; weekends, spring and fall.

Hours: Opens at 10 a.m.

Best days to attend: Monday or Tuesday.

Tickets: All day for one admission price: Adults, $9.95; ages 4–11, $8.50; under 4, free.

Other Conveniences and Attractions: Picnic facilities, camping within 10 miles, locker rentals, provisions made for handicapped, raincoats and sweatshirts for sale, lost and found, lost parents, first aid center, resting benches throughout the park, free maps of park, covered waiting areas, free parking with 1200 spaces available, most major credit cards accepted.

Other sites of interest within five miles of the park include Six Flags over Texas, International Wildlife Park, a wax museum, Texas Sports Hall of Fame, and Traders Village.

For further information write White Water Park, 701 E. Safari Parkway, Grand Prairie TX 75050, or call (214) 263-1999.

Lagoon & Pioneer Village
Farmington, Utah

Located just twenty minutes north of Salt Lake City, Lagoon & Pioneer Village is a combination amusement park and historic old-town restoration. The large restoration includes forty-two buildings, along with numerous collections and exhibits. Landscaping and park cleanliness are important aspects of the park, with over 130 people employed in these areas.

The sixty-five-acre amusement park provides thirty-two thrill rides, two visual rides, one water ride and one live animal ride, along with games, swimming, miniature golf and live entertainment. (One major news magazine has rated the Fire Dragon, Lagoon's double-loop roller coaster, as the ninth best roller coaster in the nation.) Three shops within the park provide shopping for souvenirs ranging in price from $1 to $10. Six live shows are provided in all types of theaters, from outdoor bench-seated to air-conditioned, individual-seated. Top-name entertainment occasionally performs.

Season: Weekends, April 20–May 19; daily, end of May to September.

Hours: Opens at 11 a.m.

Best day to attend: Sunday.

Tickets: All day for $12.50; or $5 admission, plus charge for each ride.

Other Conveniences and Attractions: Arcade (100 games), 10 craftsmen at work, playground area, street shows, garden walks, wildlife areas, picnic facilities, camping on premises, camera rentals, locker rentals, wheelchairs and strollers, provisions made for handicapped, raincoats and sweatshirts for sale, lost and found, lost parents, first aid center, resting benches throughout the park, free maps of park, 5000 parking spaces at a cost of $2, major credit cards accepted.

Other sites of interest are the Salt Lake City attractions.

For further information write Lagoon & Pioneer Village, P.O. Box N, Farmington UT 84025.

Saratoga
Lehi, Utah

Saratoga is a small (twenty-seven acres) water park situated on the shore of Utah Lake, midway between Salt Lake City and Provo, Utah. Picnic facilities are available on the beautifully landscaped, wooded lawns. Only one snack stand is on the premises.

Four natural warmspring swimming pools, plus six other water rides, are available. These rides include the Kamikaze waterslide (three stories high and 350 feet long), and other water slides. A boat harbor helps provide a full day of family relaxation and fun.

Season: Memorial Day through Labor Day.

Hours: Opens at 9 a.m.

Best day to attend: Any weekday.

Tickets: Charges for each ride; no admission charge.

Other Conveniences and Attractions: Arcade (20 games), playground area, garden walks, wildlife areas, picnic facilities, camping on premises, locker rentals, provisions made for handicapped, lost and found, lost parents, first aid center, resting benches throughout the park, 300 parking spaces at a cost of 50¢.

Other sites of interest nearby include Trafalga miniature Golf and Waterslide, canyons and a golf course.

For further information write Saratoga Resort, Star Route, Lehi UT 84043.

Santa's Land
Putney, Vermont

Situated on 100 acres of beautiful Vermont countryside, Santa's Land in southeastern Vermont caters mostly to families with young children and/or Christmas shoppers. The park proper is fairly small, with three amusement rides offered along with a small zoo. One restaurant offers a medium variety of meals. Visiting Santa and browsing through the many Christmas shops are the main attractions. Winter attractions also include old-fashioned sleigh rides and skiing.

Season: Year-round.

Tickets: Information not available.

Other Conveniences and Attractions: Craftsmen at work, petting zoo, garden walks, wildlife areas.

For further information write Santa's Land, Rt. 5, Putney VT 05346, or call (802) 387-5550.

Kings Dominion
Doswell, Virginia

Located in east central Virginia, just twenty miles from Richmond on I-95, this huge theme park is a close replica of its sister park in Ohio, Kings Island. The park is beautifully landscaped and well tended, with over twenty people employed specifically in landscaping and over 100 people in park maintenance (cleanliness). Along with the beautiful physical atmosphere, visitors quickly notice the friendly attitudes of the employees. Kings Dominion runs a special "positive reinforcement" program for its employees, which rewards them for friendly and courteous performance. The program works! This park was, without a doubt, one of the friendliest we visited.

Kings Dominion celebrated its tenth anniversary in 1984. Although the five theme areas' names remain the same, the attractions in each area have increased, with at least one major attraction added almost annually. 1982 brought the Grizzly roller coaster; 1983 brought the White Water Canyon ride; 1984 brought the Berserker roller coaster and the Smurfs. The park is situated on 500 acres of slightly hilly terrain, but walking is nevertheless quite easy. The park proper covers 280 acres, the safari covers 120 acres and the parking lot covers 100 acres. Most of the hills are in the ride-through safari and the parking lot areas.

Over thirty-nine major rides are offered (eleven kiddie rides), one visual ride and one live animal ride. The Safari is the major attraction in Safari Village. The other four theme areas are Hanna-Barbera Land, International Street, Old Virginia and Candy-Apple Grove. Shady Grove, another large area, is simply a beautifully landscaped rest area. Ten live shows are presented several times daily throughout the park, in all types of theaters. Top-name entertainment is quite often on the billing.

Season: Weekends, mid-March through May, and September; daily, June through August.

Hours: Opens at 9:30 a.m.

Best days to attend: Weekdays.

Tickets: All day for $13.50; 2 years and younger, free.

Other Conveniences and Attractions: Arcade (115 games plus 35 skill games), 8 craftsmen at work, street shows, garden walks, wildlife areas, picnic facilities, camping on premises and within 10 miles, pet care, camera rentals, locker rentals, wheelchairs and strollers, provisions made for handicapped, raincoats and sweatshirts for sale, lost and found and lost parents, first aid center, resting benches throughout the park, free maps of park, covered waiting areas, 8,000 parking spaces at a cost of $2, break-down service, fireworks July 2, 3 and 4, most major credit cards acccpted.

Other sites of interest nearby include Colonial Williamsburg, Washington, D.C., and more.

For further information write Kings Dominion, Doswell VA 23047, or call (804) 876-5000.

The Old Country/Busch Gardens
Williamsburg, Virginia

Located in mideastern Virginia, near Williamsburg, this 360-acre park is one of the major theme parks in the nation. Beautiful landscaping and cleanliness are evident in and between each of the eight theme areas. Approximately twenty-four people are employed to tend the 35,000 flowering plants within the park. The terrain is slightly hilly, with a couple of rather steep uphill climbs between some of the areas. There is also quite a bit of walking between the rides, but there are shows, picture-posing areas, snack concessions and plenty of resting benches along the paths.

Busch Gardens/The Old Country opened in May of 1975 next to Anheuser-Busch Brewery. Owned and operated by Busch Entertainment Corporation, it is the second largest of four parks in the corporation.

The park offers over thirty major rides and more than ten kiddie rides, among which are such famous rides as the Loch Ness Monster (double-looped intertwined coaster) and the Big Bad Wolf ($6 million free-flight coaster-thriller), new in 1984. At least one major attraction is added each year. Shopping is an adventure also, with a large range of unique and high-quality gift choices. Souvenirs range in price from $1–up. Over forty restaurants and snack concessions offer a large range of food choices, with unique menus in each of the theme areas. Over ten live shows are presented several times daily, with top-name entertainment always on the billing in one of the many theaters.

Season: Weekends, April through mid-May, September and October; daily, mid-May through August.

Hours: Opens at 10 a.m.

Tickets: All day for one admission price: $13.50 for ages 3 and up; under 3, free.

Other Conveniences and Attractions: Arcade, 10 craftsmen at work, playground area, petting zoo, street shows, garden walks, wildlife areas, camping within 10 miles, pet care, camera rentals, locker rentals, wheelchairs and strollers, provisions made for handicapped, raincoats and sweatshirts for sale, lost and found, lost parents, first aid center, resting benches throughout the park, maps of park — free and at cost, transportation from parking lot to park, transportation within the park, covered waiting areas, 2000 parking spaces at a cost of $2, break-down service, most major credit cards accepted.

Other sites of interest nearby include Washington, D.C., Kings Dominion, and much more.

For further information write The Old Country/Busch Gardens, Williamsburg VA 23187, or call (804) 253-3350.

Enchanted Village
Federal Way, Washington

Nestled amongst the trees in western Washington State, Enchanted Village is a traditional family amusement park. The trees provide plenty of shade, while the sixteen rides, two live animal rides and two water slides provide plenty of amusement.

Besides the rides, this thirty-acre park offers miniature golf, an Antique Doll and Toy Museum, a Wax Museum, wading pools and live entertainment. (One of the shows, "The Tickle Tune Typhoon," is presented on Mondays only, at the Theater in the Woods.)

Gift shops provide shopping fun, while one major restaurant and a few snack concessions offer a small range of food choices. Beautiful wooded picnicking areas are provided.

Season: Weekends, March 31 through May 19 and September; daily, mid-May through early September.

Hours: Opens at 10 a.m.

Best day to attend: Monday.

Tickets: All day for one admission price; under 3, free.

Other Conveniences and Attractions: Arcade, garden walks, petting zoo, wildlife areas, picnic facilities, free parking, antique doll and toy museum, face painting.

For further information write Enchanted Village, 36201 Kit Corner Road South, Federal Way WA 98003, or call (206) 838-8676 (Seattle) or (206) 927-9335 (Tacoma).

Camden Park
Huntington, West Virginia

Situated on twenty-five acres of flat terrain in the western part of the state, Camden Park is a traditional family amusement park that has been in operation for over eighty years. Besides the twenty-five amusement rides, the park has miniature golf, an old-fashioned riverboat ride (the Camden Queen), roller skating and a haunted house.

One shop provides souvenirs ranging in price from 50¢ to $4. A cafeteria offers a medium range of meal choices, while six snack facilities offer a slightly larger range of snack choices. Fifteen to twenty live shows are presented throughout the season, with top-name entertainment performing occasionally. Be sure to write to the park for more information about these shows.

Season: Daily, last week of April through Labor Day; weekends in April and September.

Hours: Opens at 10 a.m.

Best days to attend: Monday and Tuesday.

Tickets: 25¢ admission charge plus 10¢ tickets for rides; or all day for $6.50; senior citizens discount available.

Other Conveniences and Attractions: Arcade (35 games), picnic facilities, camping on premises and within 10 miles, wheelchairs and strollers, provisions made for handicapped, raincoats and sweatshirts for sale, lost and found, lost parents, first aid center, resting benches throughout the park, free maps of park, covered waiting areas, free parking with 50 spaces available, break-down service, fireworks on holidays.

For further information write Camden Park, P.O. Box 9245, Huntington WV 25704, or call (304) 429-4231.

Bay Beach Amusement Park
Green Bay, Wisconsin

Bay Beach Amusement Park in northeastern Wisconsin is the only amusement park we know of that is owned and operated by the city's park and recreation department for the general public. (Water-World in Dothan, Alabama is a water park owned by the city of Dothan.) The entire park is often rented out for group outings, so we suggest that you correspond with the park before planning your visit.

The small park offers eleven major amusement rides along with live pony rides. A wildlife sanctuary adjacent to Bay Beach is also operated by the park and recreation department. The two areas together cover approximately 450 acres.

One shop in the park offers souvenirs ranging in price from 10¢ to $20. One restaurant and one snack concession offer a small range of meal and snack choices. Picnicking facilities are available.

Season: Weekends, late April through May, and September; daily in June, July and August.

Hours: Opens 10 a.m.

Best days to attend: Weekdays.

Tickets: No admission charge; 10¢ per ride.

Other Conveniences and Attractions: Pony rides, arcade (22 games), playground area, petting zoo, garden walks, wildlife areas next door, picnic facilities, provisions made for handicapped, raincoats and sweatshirts for sale, lost and found, lost parents, first aid center, resting benches throughout the park, free maps of park, free parking with 800 spaces available, fireworks (occasionally).

Other sites of interest within ten miles include the wildlife sanctuary next door, the Green Bay Packers Hall of Fame and Rail America.

For further information write Bay Beach Amusement Park, 100 N. Jefferson St., Green Bay WI 54301, or call (414) 497-3677.

Pine River Amusement Park
Newton, Wisconsin

This small family amusement park, located seven miles south of Monitowoc and eleven miles north of Howards Grove on Hwy. 42, caters mostly to groups, but also provides entertainment for family outings.

The park was opened on fifteen-and-one-half acres in 1982 by Joel and Kathy Aulik, with a few rides and catering service available. Their main goal is to have a clean family park at reasonable prices. By 1988 they plan to have twelve rides and be able to offer groups a "one price for food and rides" package deal. In 1984 they were on the way with seven rides, live pony rides and miniature golf. Food services are available to groups only, although a small range of snack concessions are available in the park.

Groups currently have access to shelters, baseball diamonds, volleyball and horseshoe courts.

Season: Weekends, May, September and October; daily, June, July, August.

Hours: Opens 11 a.m.

Tickets: No admission price; each ride costs 35¢ or 3 for $1.

Other Conveniences and Attractions: Picnic facilities, camping within 10 miles, provisions made for handicapped, lost and found, first aid center, resting benches throughout the park.

For further information write Pine River Amusement Park, Rt. 2, Box 43, Newton WI 53063, or call (414) 726-4302.

Appendix I

Other Parks

Following is a list of other parks whose names we found in our research, but from which we received no information.

Alabama
Canyon Land Park
Fort Payne AL 35967

Enterprise Depot
Enterprise AL 36330

Styx River Water World
Robertsdale AL 36567

Arizona
Big Surf (water park)
1500 North Hayden Road
Tempe, Arizona 85281   (602) 947-2477

Arkansas
Booger Hollow
Dover, AR 72837

Dogpatch U.S.A.
Dogpatch, AR 72648

IQ Zoo
Hot Springs AR 71909

Mid-America Museum
Hot Springs AR 71909

Reader Railroad
Malvern AR 72104

Southland Greyhound Park
West Memphis AR 72301

Tiny Town
Hot Springs AR 71909

Wee 2 & Company
Russellville AR 72801

California
Belmont Amusement Park
8039 Beach Blvd.
Buena Park CA 90620   (714) 827-1776

Frontier Village
4885 Monterey Road
San Jose CA 95111   (408) 225-1500

Lion Country Safari
8800 Moulton Parkway
Laguna Hills CA 92653   (714) 837-1200

Marine World/Africa U.S.A.
Redwood City CA 94065   (415) 591-7676

Universal City Studio Tours   (Although not officially an
100 Universal City Plaza   amusement park, we thought
Universal City CA 91608   the address might be helpful.)

Colorado
Elitch Gardens
West 38th at Tennyson St.
Denver CO 80212   (303) 455-4771

Lakeside Amusement Park
North Sheridan at I-70
Denver CO 80212   (303) 477-1621

Physical Whimsical
3315 S. Broadway
Denver CO 80212

Connecticut
Lake Compounce Amusement Park
Lake Ave.
Bristol CT 06010   (203) 582-6333

Ocean Beach Park
New London CT 06320   (203) 447-3031

Florida
Gatorland Zoo
Kissimmee FL 32741   (305) 855-5496

Lion Country Safari
P.O. Box 16066
West Palm Beach FL 33460   (305) 793-1084

Lowry Park
Tampa FL 33612

Marco Polo Park
Bunnell FL 32018

Miracle Strip Amusement Park
12001 West Highway 98
Panama City FL 32401   (904) 234-3333

Petticoat Junction Amusement Park
Long Beach Resort
Panama City FL 32401   (904) 234-2563

Pirates World
613 East Sheridan Street
Dania FL 33004   (305) 920-7800

Wet 'N Wild
6200 International Drive
Orlando FL 32809   (305) 351-3200

Georgia
Callaway Gardens
Pine Mountain GA 31822

Lake Winnepesaukah Amusement Park
Rossville GA 30741

Lion Country Safari
Lion Country Parkway
Stockbridge GA 30281   (404) 474-1461

Stone Mountain Park
P.O. Box 778
Stone Mountain GA 30086   (404) 469-9831

The World of Sid & Marty Krofft
400 North-Omni International
Atlanta GA 30303

Hawaii
Castle Park Hawaii
4561 Salt Lake Boulevard
Honolulu HI 96818

Fernandez Fun Factory
91-246 Oihana Street
Ewa Beach HI 96706

Polynesian Cultural Center
Laie HI 96762

Illinois
Knight's Action Park
Box 204–R.R.R.
Springfield IL 62707   (217) 546-8881

Old Chicago
555 S. Bolingbrook Dr.
Bolingbrook IL 60439   (312) 759-1895

Indiana
Enchanted Forest
Mounted Route Box 386
Chesterton IN 46304   (219) 926-1614

Fun Spot Park
Lake James
200 W. County Road
Angola IN 46703   (219) 833-2972

Iowa
Adventureland
P.O. Box 3355
Des Moines IA 50316   In Iowa 1-800-532-1286

Funland Amusement Park
Arnolds Park IA 51331

Riverview Park
8th and Corning
Des Moines IA 50313   (515) 288-3621

Trainland U.S.A.
Colfax IA 50054   (515) 674-3813

Kansas
Joyland Amusement Park
2801 South Hillside
Wichita KS 67216   (316) 684-0179

Louisiana
Louisiana Purchase Gardens & Zoo Amusement Park
P.O. Box 123
Monroe LA 71210

Pontchartrain Beach Amusement Park
Lakeshore Drive at Elysian Fields
New Orleans LA 70130   (504) 288-7512

Wildlife World
Rt. 3, Box 802
Plain Dealing LA 71064   (318) 326-4164
For additional information call toll-free 1-800-535-8388; in state, call
504-925-3850.

Maine
Funland
Presque Isle Road
Caribou ME 04736   (207) 493-3157

Mariners Playland
Wells ME 04090

Thomas Point Beach & Picnic Grounds
Cook's Corner Playground
Brunswick ME 04011

Maryland
Marshall Hall Amusement Park
Route 227
Bryans Road MD 20616   (301) 743-5575

Playland Amusement Park
65th Street
Ocean City MD 21842   (301) 289-8353

Massachusetts
Lincoln Park
Route 6, State Rd.
North Dartmouth MA 02747   (617) 999-6984
Open Sunday until late June and daily to Labor Day. Some Sundays
in September.

Paragon Park
Nantasket Beach
Hull MA 02045   (617) 925-0114 or 925-0115
Open Saturday, Sunday in May. June: Monday, Wednesday, Friday,
Saturday, and Sunday until June 17th. Open daily June 17th through
Labor Day.

Salem Willows
Fort Avenue
Salem MA 01970   (617) 745-0251
Open daily May 30th to Labor Day.

Michigan
Adventure Mine
Greenland MI 49929

Cheese/Fantasyland
Pinconning MI 48650

Edgewater Park
23500 West Seven Mile Rd.
Detroit MI 48219   (313) 731-2660

Fayette Ghost Town
Garden Peninsula MI 49835

Bob-Lo Island
Detroit MI 48226   (313) 962-9622

Mississippi
Eight Flags
150 DeBuys Road
Biloxi MS 39533

Marine Life
Joseph P. Jones Park
Hwy 90
Gulfport MS 39501

Water Town
Flint Creek Water Park
Hwy 29 E
Wiggins MS 39577

Missouri
Fairyland Park
7501 Prospect Avenue
Kansas City MO 64132   (816) 333-2040

Oceans of Fun
4545 Worlds of Fun Ave.
Kansas City MO 64161

Worlds of Fun
4545 Worlds of Fun Ave.
Kansas City MO 64161   (816) 454-4545

Nebraska
Peony Park
8100 Cass Street
Omaha NE 68114   (402) 391-6253

New Hampshire
Clark's Trading Post
Lincoln NH 03251

Fantasy Farm
U.S. Route 3
Lincoln NH 03251

Santa's Village
Rt. 2
Jefferson NH 03583   (603) 586-4445

Six Gun City
Jefferson NH 03583

New Jersey
Bertrand Island Park
P.O. Box 456
Mt. Arlington NJ 07856   (201) 398-2000

Clementon Lake Park
Route 534
Clementon NJ 08021   (609) 783-0263

Vernon Valley/Great Gorge
(V&G Management Corp.)   (201) 827-2000
Vernon NJ 07462   snow phone (201) 827-3900

New York
Astroland
1000 Surf Avenue
Brooklyn NY 11224   (212) 372-0275

Crystal Beach Amusement Park
Buffalo NY 14207   (416) 894-1642

Dreamland Park — Sea Breeze
4600 Culver Road
Rochester NY 14624   (716) 467-3422

Gaslight Village
Route 9
Lake George NY 12845   (518) 792-8227

Olympic Park
1300 Scottsville Road
Rochester NY 14624   (716) 436-9180

Playland
Rye NY 10580   (914) 967-2040

Roseland Park
Lake Shore Drive
Canandaigua NY 14424   (315) 394-1140

Storytown, U.S.A.
Route 9
Lake George NY 12845   (518) 792-8802

North Carolina
Tweetsie Railroad
Blowing Rock NC 28605   (704) 295-3141

North Dakota
Rough Rider Time Machine
Medora ND 58645

Ohio
Americana Amusement Park
5757 Middletown-Hamilton Rd.
Middletown OH 45042   (513) 539-7339

Chippewa Lake
Chippewa Lake OH 44215   (216) 769-2481

Columbus Zoo Amusement Park
Box 398
Grove City OH 43123   (614) 871-0170 or 889-5055

Fantasy Farm Amusement Park
5855 Hamilton-Middletown Rd.
Middletown OH 45042   (513) 539-8864

Fun Country Action Park
P.O. Box 477
Cambridge OH 43725   (614) 432-3565

Putt 'N Pond Park
21254 S.R. 12
Fostoria OH 44830   (419) 435-9568

Oklahoma
Bell's Amusement Park
21st and New Haven
Tulsa OK 74114   (918) 932-1991

Springlake Amusement Park
1800 Springlake Dr.
Oklahoma City OK 73111   (405) 424-1405

Oregon
The Oaks Amusement Park
Sellwood Bridge
Portland OR 97202   (503) 233-5777

Pennsylvania
Bushkill Park
Easton PA 18042

Cascade Park
New Castle PA 16101

Hansen's Amusement Park
Harvey's Lake PA 18618

Idlewild Park
Ligonier PA 15658

Lakemont Park
Altoona PA 16601

Lakewood Park
Barnesville PA 18214

Magic Valley Park
Bushkill PA 18324

Main Line Park
West Chester PA 19380

Nay Aug Amusement Co.
Scranton PA 18510

Rocky Glen Park
Avoca PA 18641

Sesame Place
Langhorne PA 19047

Story Book Forest
Ligonier PA 15658

Waldemeer Beach Park
Erie PA 16515

West Point Park
West Point PA 19486

White Swan Park
Coraopolis PA 15108

Williams Grove Park
Mechanicsburg PA 17055

Rhode Island
The Enchanted Forest
Rt. 3
Hopkinton RI 02833　　　　　　　(401) 539-7711

Rocky Point Park
Rocky Point Ave.
Warwick RI 02886　　　　　　　(401) 737-8000

Slater Memorial Park & Zoo
U.S. Rt. 1-A
Pawtucket RI 02860

South Carolina
Crescent Beach Pavilion and Amusements
17th Ave. North
North Myrtle Beach SC 29582

Grand Strand Amusement Park
4th Avenue & S. Ocean Blvd.
Myrtle Beach SC 29577

Myrtle Beach Pavilion
812 N. Ocean Blvd.
Myrtle Beach SC 29577

Ocean Drive Pavilion and Amusement Park
Main St. & Ocean Blvd.
North Myrtle Beach SC 29582

Sun Fun Amusement Park
Main St. & U.S. 17
North Myrtle Beach SC 29582

Surfside Amusement Park
Surfside Beach SC 29577

Tennessee
Lake Winnepesaukah
Off U.S. Highway 27, South
Chattanooga TN 37041   (404) 866-5681

Silver Dollar City
P.O. Box 928
Pigeon Forge TN 37863   (615) 453-4616

Texas
Alamo Village Vacationland
P.O. Box 528
Brackettville TX 78832   (512) 563-2580

Aquarena Springs
P.O. Box 2330
San Marcos TX 78666   (512) 392-2481

Sea-Arama Marineworld
91st and Seawall Blvd., P.O. Box 3068
Galveston TX 77552   (713) 744-4501

Sesame Place
Hwy. 183 at Esters Rd. Exit
Irving TX 75061   (212) 445-0485

State Fair Park
Dallas TX 75226   (214) 823-9931

Wild River Canyon
P.O. Box 8529
Midland TX 79703   (915) 694-0505

Wonder World
P.O. Box 1369
San Marcos TX 78666   (512) 392-6711

Wonderland Park
(Thompson Park)
Hwy. 287 North & 24th St.
Amarillo TX 79107

Utah
Saltair Resort
Salt Lake City UT 84119

Vermont
Alpine Slides:
  Pico Alpine Slide
  Sherburne Pass
  Rutland VT 05701   (802) 775-4345

  Alpine Slide at Spruce Peak
  Route 108
  Mansfield VT   (802) 253-7311

  Bromley Alpine Slide
  Rt. 11
  Manchester VT   (802) 824-5522

Virginia
Lakeside Amusement Park
1526 E. Main St.
Salem VA 24153   (703) 366-8871

Washington
Fun Forest
Seattle Center
Seattle WA 98109   (206) 624-1585

Riverfront Park
507 North Howard Street
Spokane WA 99201   (509) 456-5511 or 5518

Wisconsin
Dandelion Park
Muskego WI 53105   (414) 679-2400

Appendix II

Other Sites of Interest

A few other sites of interest around each park have been listed, wherever possible, within the descriptions of the parks. As it would be difficult, if not impossible, to list *all* sites of interest around each park, we suggest that you obtain more detailed information by writing to the state's Bureau of Tourism in that state's capital city, as listed below:

Montgomery AL 36119
Juneau AK 99802
Phoenix AZ 85026
Little Rock AR 72231
Sacramento CA 95813
Denver CO 80212
Hartford CT 06101
Dover DE 19903
Tallahassee FL 32301
Atlanta GA 30304
Honolulu HI 96818
Boise ID 83708
Springfield IL 62707
Indianapolis IN 46206
Des Moines IA 50316
Topeka KS 66603
Frankfort KY 40601
Baton Rouge LA 70821
Augusta ME 04333
Annapolis MD 21401
Boston MA 02205
Lansing MI 48924

Saint Paul MN 55101
Jackson MS 39205
Jefferson City MO 65102
Helena MT 59601
Lincoln NE 68501
Carson City NV 89702
Concord NH 03301
Trenton NJ 08601
Santa Fe NM 87501
Albany NY 12212
Raleigh NC 27611
Bismarck ND 58502
Columbus OH 43216
Oklahoma City OK 73125
Salem OR 97301
Harrisburg PA 17105
Providence RI 02940
Columbia SC 29201
Pierre SD 57501
Nashville TN 37214
Austin TX 78710
Salt Lake City UT 84119

Montpelier VT 05602
Richmond VA 23232
Olympia WA 98501
Charleston WV 25301
Madison WI 53707
Cheyenne WY 82001

Index